Who Should Pay for **Medicare?**

Daniel Shaviro

Who Should Pay for *Medicare?*

The University of Chicago Press

Chicago and London

DANIEL SHAVIRO is professor of law at New York University
School of Law. He is author of *Do Deficits Matter?* (1997),
*When Rules Change: An Economic and Political Analysis of
Transition Relief and Retroactivity* (2000), and *Making Sense
of Social Security Reform* (2000), all published by the
University of Chicago Press.

The University of Chicago Press, Chicago 60637
The University of Chicago Press, Ltd., London
© 2004 by The University of Chicago
All rights reserved. Published 2004
Printed in the United States of America

13 12 11 10 09 08 07 06 05 04   1 2 3 4 5
ISBN: 0-226-75076-0 (cloth)

Library of Congress Cataloging-in-Publication Data

Shaviro, Daniel N.
    Who should pay for Medicare? / Daniel Shaviro.
        p. ; cm.
    Includes bibliographical references and index.
        ISBN 0-226-75076-0 (cloth : alk. paper)
        1. Medicare—Economic aspects. 2. Medicare—Finance.
3. Medical care, Cost of—United States. 4. Health care reform—
United States.
        [DNLM: 1. Medicare—economics. 2. Health Care Reform—
economics. 3. United States. WT 31 S538w 2004] I. Title.

RA412.3 .S53 2004
338.4'3368426'00973—dc21

                                        2003012964

For Pat, Peter, and Charles

CONTENTS

Suppose a car dealer were to approach you and ask, "Would you like a new car?" If you were to answer the question literally, you would almost have to say yes. After all, there is bound to be something nice about having a new car.

You surely would realize, however, that the dealer was actually asking you something rather different: "Do you want to buy a new car from me?" Here, even if the dealer had the right car and could be talked into a reasonable price, it is possible that your answer would be no. It all depends on whether you happen to want a new car badly enough to be willing to pay the price.

Unfortunately, in the context of Washington politics, this elementary point, which every consumer understands, verges on being a revelation. We give deserving or politically powerful groups, and above all seniors, huge and costly benefits that they do not have to pay for, rationalized on the ground that the benefits are nice. We do not seriously ask whether the benefits are worth their cost, or whether it is fair to transfer wealth from the payers—and there always must be payers, even if we simply run up the federal debt rather than identifying them promptly—to the beneficiaries.

This book seeks to lend balance and perspective to the discussion of Medicare—already the second-largest government program, after Social Security, and potentially on a path toward becoming the largest. The question the book asks—who should pay for Medicare or, more precisely, for seniors' healthcare—could hardly be more timely. On November 25, 2003, Congress passed the biggest new entitlement in nearly forty years, since Medicare itself was enacted, by adding an unfunded prescription drug benefit to the program.

Should seniors get prescription drugs? Surely it's desirable that they, and also younger people, receive necessary healthcare without being wiped out financially. Should Medicare include a prescription drug benefit? Surely any well-designed healthcare program that spends more than $200 billion per year would carry such a benefit in its package, since prescription drugs are a vital part of modern medical treatment. But should we have added an unfunded benefit that is conservatively projected to cost

$400 billion in the first ten years after enactment, and probably more than $1 trillion in the ten years after that? That is a very different question, just as in the case of the car dealer.

There are two big problems with passing such a benefit at this time in our history, even assuming for the moment that the benefit is otherwise well designed. The first problem is that it is Robin Hood in reverse, giving money to affluent seniors at the expense, in many cases, of poorer workers. It vastly increases the already huge wealth redistribution through our fiscal system from younger to older generations, in violation of the age-old covenant urging beneficence by each generation toward its children and grandchildren. We have passed, with scarcely any discussion of what we were doing, what Republican Senator Judd Gregg calls "the largest tax increase one generation has put on another generation in the history of this country," contrived simply to "get us through the next election."

The second big problem is that our current budgetary policy does not even remotely suggest how this benefit can be paid for. Annual budget deficits that already are projected to reach half a trillion dollars per year will only continue to grow as baby boomers retire, life expectancies rise, and expensive new wonder drugs (wonderful at least in their marketing) are discovered. Yet the George W. Bush administration, which gave us (through its control of Congress) the new prescription drug benefit, keeps on slashing taxes and raising government spending almost across the board without the slightest concern about our fiscal future. Democrats, meanwhile, complain that the new prescription drug benefit is not generous enough.

The design of the new prescription drug benefit almost ensures that it will soon be expanded. True insurance provides people with coverage against worst-case scenarios, such as having to pay a lot for healthcare when they become gravely ill. It does not offer first-dollar coverage of routine expenses; this would merely encourage waste and serve as a handout to anyone who received the coverage without having to pay for it. But true insurance is not politically popular, because if you lose your insurance "bet" by not actually having a catastrophe that would trigger its coverage, you may complain, after the fact, that you didn't get anything out of it.

So the prescription drug benefit has been given, in common with preexisting Medicare, a partly upside-down insurance structure whereby, after paying a $250 deductible, enrollees without other prescription drug coverage get the following government payments:

—75 percent coverage for the first $2,000 (above the deductible) that they spend on covered prescription drugs,

—no coverage for the next $2,850 that they spend, and

—95 percent of everything they spend beyond that.

The last of these three coverage brackets admittedly is true insurance. But the first really is not, and once it has been granted the second stands out like a sore thumb, already dubbed the "donut hole" by Washington insiders. You can bet that efforts to eliminate it and offer at least 75 percent coverage throughout will commence immediately.

Some seniors have begun to complain that the new benefit is stingy. Implicit in this complaint is the expectation that, whenever seniors face financial difficulty, they will receive a well-deserved handout. This expectation is encouraged both by the genuine financial and medical challenges that many of them face and by decades of political pandering to seniors, both affluent and needy. So the expansion of this benefit is already beginning to seem like water running downhill.

Now, perhaps the handout is well deserved, although so would be handouts to needy younger people who will be helping to pay for the benefits. Lots of us, perhaps all of us, would like more than we can realistically have without unfairly depriving others. But Medicare should not be thought of as a handout. The real point of Medicare is to provide universal health insurance coverage at a certain stage in life. And, like any insurance system, it must have enough funds coming in to pay for the benefits that it metes out.

The recent budget policies of the president and Congress, including enactment of the prescription drug benefit in its current form, are so irresponsible that they verge on fiscal treason. If we do not change course, these policies are highly likely to cause, within ten to fifteen years, a fiscal meltdown like those that have recently plagued nations such as Brazil and Argentina, complete with hyperinflation, rising unemployment, and recurrent bank failures. We like to think that our economy is too strong for this to happen, but if our policies are foolish enough for long enough, it can and will happen.

Recent estimates of the fiscal gap—that is, the amount, in today's dollars, by which we fall short of being able to meet our future commitments—range from $44 trillion to $74 trillion. To get a sense of what this means, suppose that the U.S. Treasury tried today to sell from $44 trillion to $74 trillion worth of bonds on world capital markets, while cheerfully announcing that taxes should still be cut and that no significant government spending cuts were imminent. The main difference between this and our actual present situation is simply that, as things stand, the bond markets haven't fully caught on yet to the fact that this is where we are headed, or else are hoping against hope (and against the evidence) that grown-ups will soon take the helm.

Can we grow out of the fiscal gap if the economy takes off again? Unfortunately, no. Social Security and Medicare, which together are responsible for more than 100 percent of the fiscal gap (since everything else is roughly in long-term budgetary balance), are both effectively pegged to the size of the economy. The bigger it gets, the bigger they get. So, while economic growth is certainly something to hope for, it does not actually make the fiscal gap go away. Indeed, the opposite happens. At some point, the fiscal gap is likely to start choking off economic growth, by requiring tax increases on current workers so as to keep the benefits to seniors flowing. This will reduce our already low national saving rate, possibly making it negative, and make the prospects for vigorous economic growth a lot dimmer than they would otherwise be.

What can we do to stave off the misfortunes toward which our political leaders, in response to the evident demands of our voters, are leading us? In this book, I offer both recommendations and a more pessimistic set of predictions. The former include tax increases and such changes to Medicare as reduced coverage of routine expenditures and greater use of income-related charges to enrollees. The latter include price controls and increased queuing, which would make Medicare a second-class program, and a real possibility of Weimar Germany–style hyperinflation. One big difference between the recommendations and the predictions has to do with timing. Current seniors ought to share the burden with younger generations, which requires acting sooner rather than later, but our distorted politics makes it unlikely that they will.

More important than my specific recommendations and predictions is the way of looking at Medicare and other government programs that I suggest. A public economics perspective, rooted in the understanding that there is no free lunch, that every distributional winner implies a distributional loser, and that incentives matter, is hardly novel in the academy, but it has been too little heard in public policy debate. If nothing else, I hope to do my bit, through this book, to improve our political discourse and thus help to create the preconditions for a more rational policy. Even seniors and ardent "social insurance" advocates—whose sympathies, in many respects, I share—will, I hope, get the message that the time for being fair and responsible without grave disruption of our political and economic life is rapidly growing short.

ACKNOWLEDGMENTS

I am grateful to Anne Alstott, Sherry Glied, workshop participants at New York University School of Law and the University of Michigan Law School, and two anonymous reviewers for their helpful comments on earlier drafts.

Introduction

EVERYONE agrees about the need for Medicare reform. Everyone, that is, except the voters, along with politicians who prefer adding costly new benefits, such as prescription drug coverage, to a program that already has unfunded commitments that could reasonably be estimated at $46 trillion. So perhaps it is more accurate to say that everyone agrees about the need for Medicare reform, except for almost everyone.

Still, because anything that must happen ultimately will happen, Medicare reform can be expected at some point. The system in its present form is fiscally unsustainable, in part for demographic reasons, but also due to the ongoing development of welcome yet costly new medical technologies. Over the next seventy-five years, its expenditures are expected to grow by 400 percent relative to the economy, while its current revenue sources grow scarcely faster than the economy. Achieving long-term fiscal stability for Medicare might therefore require changes on the order of an immediate 40 percent benefit cut or 60 percent revenue increase. So the system will at some point change because it must. Public sentiment cannot indefinitely derail Medicare reform any more than it could keep the tide from rising.

Two types of issues need to be resolved in retooling Medicare for the twenty-first century. The first, reflecting its impact on healthcare delivery, is who should make various choices about a given enrollee's covered care. The second, reflecting that Medicare is a fiscal system, is who should pay for the care.

The issues of who chooses and who pays are closely linked, given how financial incentives affect decisions. Yet they turn on different types of information. The "who chooses" question requires detailed institutional knowledge about the healthcare industry—for example, concerning how providers' preferences and incentives would operate in different settings, and how well consumers can decide about their own care. The "who pays" question turns on distributional and efficiency issues of the same kind as those raised by the income tax, welfare, and Social Security systems.

To date, Medicare has mainly been the intellectual province of health-care experts who have valuable specialized knowledge about the "who chooses" issues. The system has not received as much attention from "who pays" experts—frightened off, perhaps, by all the arcana of modern healthcare institutions. Yet, in some respects, Medicare is merely Social Security with a twist, providing as it does retirement benefits that are financed on a roughly pay-as-you-go basis by taxes on current workers. Even the main difference—that the benefits are provided in-kind rather than in cash—has analogues elsewhere in the fiscal system, such as in choosing between cash and other transfers (including Food Stamps, rent subsidies, Medicaid, and education vouchers) to the poor.

A public economics perspective therefore has a great deal to add to the Medicare debate. Although the "who chooses" issues are important, questions of who pays are important too. Their resolution (or nonresolution) will play a critical role in Medicare's success or failure in the decades ahead. They ought, therefore, to be examined with the same care that the "who chooses" issues have been getting for some time. Such an examination should interest not only those whose healthcare expertise it complements, but many generalists who care about public policy but have previously found Medicare forbidding due to the specialized terminology that unavoidably pervades sophisticated "who chooses" discussions.

There are three main contributions I aim to make by applying a public economics perspective to Medicare. The first is to offer an analytical framework for understanding what it does as a fiscal system, based on subdividing it into its distinct conceptual parts. The second is to explain and place in perspective the system's long-term fiscal gap. The third is to offer a set of suggestions for addressing its financing problems in as equitable and efficient (albeit inevitably painful) a manner as possible.

Breaking Down Medicare into Its Parts

Medicare is a multipurpose system, and proposals to change it may have multiple types of effects. A failure to separate these out can turn the reform debate into a game of blindman's buff, where choices for rationalizing the program are off-limits simply because they have not been clearly understood. This is an area where we often do not really have a clear sense of what we are talking about. Medicare is enshrouded in myth, not only by the grace of its history as the one Great Society enactment to share the New Deal's rosy halo, but also by the sheer inscrutability of when and how it redistributes lifetime income, rather than merely returning to enrollees the value of their own tax contributions. This inscrutability, by making retirees' benefits seem at once earned and yet a bonanza, has long helped make Medicare, even more than Social Security, politically sacred—a status that is denied to more transparent portions of our fiscal system, such as the income tax and pork barrel spending.

Thus, in evaluating who should pay for Medicare—or more precisely, for seniors' healthcare[1]—it helps to break things down a bit. Medicare, in a sense, is two distinct programs wrapped together: a retirement program for all Americans and a national healthcare system for seniors. Each of these programs can then be further broken down into component subprograms that raise distinct issues and could be separately redesigned. In particular, the retirement program serves three different functions. The first is forced saving, insofar as you cannot spend in advance the value of the retirement benefits that it offers. The second is limiting portfolio choice regarding how to save the accruing value of these benefits. (You cannot, for example, choose stock market investment in the hope of getting a higher albeit riskier expected return.) The third function is redistribution, insofar as some people get benefits worth more than the time-adjusted value of their tax contributions, while others get less.

The biggest winners from Medicare redistribution have been older generations at the expense of the younger. In addition, though on a much smaller scale, Medicare transfers wealth from single individuals and two-earner couples to one-earner married couples. It has not, however, resulted in significant (if any) progressive redistribution within age cohorts, even though high-earners pay greater income and payroll taxes for what is nominally the same coverage. The greater taxes are offset by greater benefits, due to high-earners' not only living longer but generally getting more intensive treatment than low-earners for the same medical condition (McClellan and Skinner 1997, 25).

This lack of progressivity may come as a surprise to most people, although it is hard to be sure since Medicare seems to be viewed both as redistributive and yet (despite the inconsistency) as giving each retiree benefits that she has paid for. To be sure, no matter how much (or little) progressivity one prefers, there is no inherent reason why Medicare itself must be progressive. What matters, presumably, is the effect of our fiscal system as a whole. Yet Medicare's possibly misunderstood lack of progressivity should be kept in mind when we consider how to make it fiscally sustainable.

Medicare's national healthcare system for seniors, like its retirement program, can be decomposed conceptually—in this case, into two parts. The first provides health insurance coverage, while the second provides payment for a specific set of healthcare benefits. These subprograms are inevitably associated, since offering either one necessarily implies providing the other, but to some extent the issues they raise are distinct.

Medicare's agreed purpose is to provide "social insurance" by guaranteeing seniors adequate healthcare treatment. We will see that the notion of "social insurance" has multiple relevant dimensions, some of which the current system performs better than others. To some extent, Medicare provides not insurance in the strict economic sense of risk-spreading, but risk prevention through limits on individual choice. Consider automobile accident risks, which we partly address through speed limits and seatbelt rules, and by saying that children and people under the influence of alcohol cannot drive. Similarly, Medicare prevents you from entering retirement uninsured and with too little saving to afford retirement healthcare.

"Insurance" in a strict economic sense refers to spreading or pooling risk across a large population. Thus, a group of automobile drivers may pool their accident risks (typically with an insurance company acting as the intermediary) so that anyone who has an accident will not be financially ruined. In effect, each participant bets against herself as a driver, since she only gets paid if she has a costly accident. This need not, however, reflect pessimism about one's luck or skill as a driver. Instead, the insured may aim to shift the money she can command among different possible future states of the world, so that she will have more in those states where she anticipates a greater need for it. If, however, one driver agreed or was compelled to pay in full for another's accidents along with her own, this would not be true insurance in an aggregate social sense (although the benefited driver would presumably regard herself as insured). Risk would only have been shifted, not diffused.

As we will see, in some respects Medicare is a true risk-spreading system. Consider its mandating health insurance without the risk-based premiums that private insurers may demand, thereby addressing the risks of being either sick or at high risk of getting sick. In other respects, however, Medicare merely transfers risk from one group of participants to another. Thus, consider the risk that the average retirement healthcare needs for a given age cohort will increase as technological advances make new kinds of treatment possible. (While such advances are good for you if they mean you will get better care, they are worth insuring against in the sense that they increase the marginal value to you of a retirement dollar.) Rather than spreading this risk, Medicare generally just transfers it to the future generations that will bear the fiscal cost of increased utilization of the program, notwithstanding that the same technological advances may cause retirement saving to be more valuable to them as well.

Even where Medicare does spread risk, it is in some respects poorly designed to do so. The character of the optimal insurance contract depends on the trade-off between the *benefit* of hedging the underlying risks (such as of sickness or fire) that the contract offsets and the *cost* of its adverse effect on your incentives, since you may be less assiduous about minimizing costs that the insurance company, rather than you, will bear.

Medicare is structured to provide a lot of coverage for routine medical expenses, thereby substantially reducing consumers' cost consciousness without providing significant risk-spreading. At the same time, it fails to provide high-end coverage for those who end up needing catastrophic or long-term care. It thereby gets the insurance wrong on both ends, concentrating its coverage where the incentive problems are greatest and the hedging benefits slightest.

Causes of Medicare's Long-Term Fiscal Gap

While Medicare's upside-down insurance structure surely contributes to its fiscal gap, no one thinks that turning it right-side-up would help nearly enough. Nor could one restore its long-term solvency simply through greater regulatory efforts at curbing the proverbial waste, fraud, and abuse. The underlying problem is more structural. It reflects Medicare's initial design as what may once have seemed to be a truly sustainable, non-exploding variant of a Ponzi scheme. (An example of a Ponzi scheme is an illegal chain letter where the originator asks eight people to send her a dollar and each then asks the same of eight more people, ostensibly continuing forever.)

Medicare shares with Ponzi schemes the idea of having the first group of participants get benefits for free, with the resulting liability being rolled over indefinitely. Yet it also differs from them in an important way. Rather than requiring an exponential increase in participants, all it requires to be indefinitely sustainable is demographic and a certain kind of technological stability. So long as the ratios of workers to retirees and covered healthcare expenditure to gross domestic product (GDP) remain constant, the program can just keep going indefinitely.

With demographic stability, as Paul Samuelson (1958) first explained with regard to Social Security, each generation after the lucky initiators (who get their retirement support for free) receives a positive return on its tax contributions, with the rate of return depending on productivity growth in the workforce. In the Medicare setting, if healthcare expenditures remain in lockstep with GDP, retirees can use the funds they receive to pay for retirement healthcare that is unchanging in its adequacy relative to contemporaneous treatment norms, yet ever-improving in absolute terms if the economy keeps growing and medical technology keeps improving.

Alas, these seemingly simple preconditions of demographic and technological stability have evaporated for the foreseeable future due to two ongoing shocks to the system. The first is increasing life expectancies, driven by some combination of improved healthcare technology and "changes in diet, smoking, exercise, and other aspects of personal behavior" (Fuchs 1984, 6). This is a more significant factor, in lowering worker to retiree ratios, than the aging of the baby boom generation. The second shock is costly yet valuable advances in healthcare technology that have improved treatment outcomes in many settings but caused medical expenditure to grow faster than the economy.

These two fiscally adverse trends are actually good things—the kinds of "shocks" that every society might like to have. Who would not welcome living longer and getting ever better medical treatment? Yet, welcome though they may be, they are trends that one ought to "insure" against. Money is more valuable to you in states of the world where you will be retired for longer and more able to benefit from costly medical treatment.

With hindsight, Medicare's pay-as-you-go financing structure was imprudent after all (even if not at the Ponzi level), given the financing risks that came to pass and the foreseeable slowness of the political system to respond to them adequately. Yet looking forward is more important than regretting or criticizing the past. So the question of real importance is what to do about Medicare's fiscal gap. Before turning to this, however, we should first look more closely at why the fiscal gap might matter.

Significance of Medicare's Long-Term Fiscal Gap

In a sense, Medicare's long-term fiscal gap actually means less than meets the eye. To say that the program is in long-term deficit is to say that, under announced policy, its expected expenditures exceed its expected revenues. Over the long run, then, Medicare's announced policy cannot be its actual policy, given what economists call the "intertemporal budget constraint": you can only spend what you have, and everything must ultimately be paid for (the no-free-lunch principle). This, of course, is an idea that one need not be an economist to understand. Anyone with a bank account or a family budget to manage ought to grasp it as well.

It is worth asking, however, why should we care if the announced policy is not the actual policy. Doesn't this simply mean that, at some point, the announced policy will have to change? Why worry about delay in announcing the true policy?

As we will see, the problems with Medicare's fiscal gap are several. People may plan poorly if they misunderstand the likely future. In the private realm, this might involve saving too little for one's own retirement. In the public realm, it involves ignoring trade-offs between, say, tax cuts and prescription drug benefits today and what Medicare or other government programs will be able to provide in the future. Postponing the announcement day also may adversely affect future generations, which will have to bear all of the eventual tax cuts or spending increases if we do nothing. Thus, the Medicare fiscal gap benefits the old at the expense of the young or as yet unborn without requiring explicit acknowledgment that this is the policy.

Medicare Financing versus the Overall Budget Picture

Since Medicare is merely one government program among many, its fiscal gap would not justify concern if, in the rest of the budget, revenues sufficiently exceeded outlays. Were that the case, the only needed policy change would be to increase the proportion of general revenues that go to Medicare. Unfortunately, however, the overall federal budget has an even greater projected fiscal gap than Medicare standing alone. Using assumptions similar to those that underlie an estimated Medicare fiscal gap of $46 trillion, the overall fiscal gap in the federal budget can be estimated at $74 trillion. And while this number is extremely soft and imprecise, susceptible to changing substantially in response to new information or altered (but still reasonable) assumptions, it seems considerably more likely to go up than down in the current political climate.

The Medicare Trust Fund that keeps track of revenues and expenditures attributed to one of the program's official parts (concerning hospital insurance) provides a bit of an early warning system concerning the long-term fiscal picture. So does the Social Security Trust Fund. However, the Trust Fund computations fall considerably short of offering an accurate picture. Moreover, the fact that they are made on a separate-system basis can encourage Congress to adopt smoke-and-mirrors responses that call off the early warning without addressing the fiscal gap. Examples might include restating official Trust Fund balances or reshuffling the manner in which various revenues or expenditures are officially recorded. The political predilection to look at Medicare's finances in a vacuum, and thus to consider mere smoke-and-mirrors fixes, is so pervasive that a brief story is in order to dramatize the issue and provide a useful catchphrase.

Mr. and Mrs. Clown—the Clown family—are hard workers but not the best financial planners. They run a corner grocery store, organized as a proprietorship from which they take all profits and are liable to pay all debts. They realize that the store is losing money and that their savings are therefore starting to dwindle.

"What can we do?" Mr. Clown asks.

Mrs. Clown replies, "Of course we're losing money! What do you expect when you consider that we've been working for free? We need to start paying ourselves a decent living wage."

So they start paying themselves $2,500 a month each, and consider themselves lucky to have found such good workers who would work for so little. The salary is nice, but then they notice that the grocery store is losing $5,000 a month more than previously. What to do now? Hard times demand belt-tightening all around. So they hold a workers' meeting, and, once they have explained it all to themselves, reluctantly agree to accept a temporary paycut.

Ultimately, Mr. and Mrs. Clown go bankrupt, and thus learn the hard way about the importance of looking at the entire budgetary picture. Yet their response to the family fiscal crisis did not actually hurt, apart from distracting their attention. It merely failed to help, since salary is a wash if you pay it to yourself.

I henceforth use the term "Clown family accounting" to describe this sort of myopia, whereby one mistakes a part of one's finances for the whole and thus erroneously views a shift between the parts as significant. To be sure, Clown family accounting has very different implications for the federal government than for the Clowns. It betokens not bankruptcy, since the government can always raise taxes or walk away from commitments that are not legally binding, but simply a failure to choose intelligently between priorities. For example, if mere bookkeeping changes in the revenues or expenditures attributed to Medicare lead to the postponement of any genuine response, we will still ultimately face the same overall fiscal gap, only with less advance warning and fewer options. And if we choose a particular change to Medicare simply because we are fixated on the program's official accounting, we may miss the chance to ask more fundamentally how we want to share benefits and burdens among our citizens.

Paying for Medicare

Closing the fiscal gap, both Medicare's and the larger one, is likely to require changes on both the expenditure and revenue sides. To a large extent, the question of how best to cut Medicare expenditures requires a detailed understanding of the healthcare industry. The aim, after all, is to target relatively wasteful expenditure, raising the issue of who should decide, given that medical needs are hard to judge and that none of the players (such as patients, doctors, and insurers) has entirely the right incentives. This, in turn, requires considering such matters as how providers respond to Medicare's pricing structure, and whether Medicare should pursue the cost savings that private sector insurers have sought from replacing unsupervised fee-for-service coverage with managed care. Important though these issues are, I mainly leave them, for reasons of comparative advantage, to the healthcare experts.

Public economics can, however, help in evaluating everything on the revenue side, including not just taxes but Medicare copayments that may affect healthcare expenditures. Moreover, public economics (and welfare economics) can help to illuminate the philosophical question, critical to Medicare policy, of how differences in health status, alongside those pertaining to such attributes as lifetime earnings, gender, life expectancy, and date of birth, should affect societal wealth distribution.

In addressing the fiscal gap, I argue that net revenues should be increased sooner rather than later, both to restrain current generations from leaving too little for their own retirement and to aid future generations. A variety of fiscal instruments could be used, in some respects interchangeably, toward this end. Our choices, however, should reflect both the fundamental issue of who ought to pay and the crasser, more opportunistic question of what is likely to be politically feasible.

My principal conclusions include the following:

(1) Income and payroll taxes, as the main instruments in the U.S. fiscal system for distributing burdens based on some measure of ability to pay, are obvious candidates to play a major role in narrowing the fiscal gap. Any increases may be hard to enact in the near term, however. Moreover, even if they were enacted, Congress might be likely to dissipate the net revenues, since immediate gratification is more rewarding than saving to meet future needs. A variety of official budgetary conventions might be used to try to combat this tendency (Clown family accounting, but in a good cause), but with uncertain prospects for success.

(2) Reducing or eliminating the existing income tax exclusion for employer-provided health insurance would aid Medicare wholly apart from its being a tax increase. The income tax exclusion gives employees an incentive to overinsure, even if it results in wasteful expenditure that increases the cost of their coverage. When current workers and their families therefore join Medicare enrollees in being non–cost conscious, the entire healthcare industry is affected. Medical treatment norms and medical technology firms' research agendas evolve against a background of limited cost

consciousness, thus contributing to rising healthcare costs that we all bear not just directly as consumers, but also through Medicare as taxpayers.

(3) Current seniors ought not to be uniquely exempted from sharing in the pain that younger Americans must bear in narrowing the fiscal gap. Yet, if retired, they are past the point where they can be much affected by income and payroll tax increases. One politically convenient way to make them pay their share would be to enact a value-added tax (VAT) on consumption, perhaps with some gesture toward earmarking revenues to pay for Medicare benefits. A VAT may function on enactment as a one-time wealth tax (borne in large part by the elderly because they hold so much of our wealth). While this may have distortionary effects that are comparable to those from a fully pre-announced tax, there may be no better way of helping to pay for Medicare.

(4) Seniors also ought to be required to bear increased copayments for routine expenditures. This would increase cost consciousness in addition to narrowing the fiscal gap. Increased cost-sharing could perhaps be made less politically unpalatable by mingling it, as a matter of political presentation, with more popular changes to address gaps in Medicare's coverage.

(5) Cost-sharing by Medicare enrollees should increase with some measure of their means, to mitigate the burden on seniors who are less well-off. Taxable income, modified by the exclusion of wages up to a ceiling (to limit incentives to retire), might be used as the means test. Even if means-testing undermined Medicare's political appeal as an ostensibly "universal" program, this would not be all to the bad, since at present political support for the program is, if anything, too strong relative to the support for competing priorities.

Roadmap for the Rest of This Book

The book is organized as follows. Chapter 2 describes the key features of the current Medicare system, exploring the benefits it provides, how it is financed, and the significance (which we will see is close to nil) of the official Medicare Trust Funds. Chapter 3 discusses Medicare's incentive and distributional effects. Chapter 4 decomposes Medicare into its constitutive elements reflecting its character as a retirement system for all Americans and as a national healthcare system for enrollees. Chapter 5 discusses the social insurance issues raised by Medicare and proposals for its reform. Chapters 6 and 7 turn to Medicare's fiscal gap, discussing first the underlying reasons for it and then its significance. Chapters 8–10 discuss Medicare reform options pertaining in turn to healthcare benefits, enrollee contributions, and taxes to narrow the fiscal gap. Chapter 11 offers conclusions and predictions.

Medicare Today: Key Features of the Current System

What Do People Like about Medicare?

"MEND IT, don't end it" is the harshest thing most Americans would say about Medicare, which remains "one of the nation's most popular social programs" (Oberlander 2003, 147). And "mend it" principally means add new benefits without new financing. It is not hard to see why Medicare is so popular—making it, even more than Social Security, the "third rail of American politics: touch it and you die" (Epstein 1999, 147). It offers free healthcare at the point of service, thus providing something for nothing once you have reached retirement. Moreover, while current and past enrollees are presumably well aware of having paid Medicare taxes, this has not been overly onerous, since "lifetime payments by current beneficiaries have never come close to financing their lifetime expenditures" (McClellan and Skinner 1997, 5).

There may be no free lunches globally, but there are plenty to be had locally, and those who get them are likely to be glad of it. Yet popular support for Medicare rests on more than either the global free lunch fallacy or the local free lunch reality. People may say: "I am glad that I will be aided when I am old and face high medical expenses that I can no longer earn the money to pay for. Whether I ended up lacking the personal resources out of bad luck in the 'health lottery,' or because I never earned enough to save for my retirement care, or even through pure misjudgment of my foreseeable medical needs, I would value the health security that Medicare seems to offer me."

This ground for liking Medicare is nothing to sneer at. In a nutshell, it explains why we might sensibly want to ensure that all retirees have adequate health insurance (the basic Medicare aim). Yet, no matter how strongly we endorse this aim, no judgment immediately follows about the merits, as compared to possible alternatives, of the actual Medicare system. Such a judgment requires closer consideration of exactly how Medicare implements the health security idea. This chapter lays the foundation for a fuller assessment of Medicare by examining the program's main attributes.

What benefits does it provide (and omit)? How does it fit into the landscape of related federal healthcare programs? How is it paid for?

The Benefits Side

Medicare provides coverage not only for people over age sixty-five, but also for those who are disabled or have end-stage renal disease. This book, however, considers only its senior coverage (except that some quoted statistics relate to the entire program). Medicare's disability and end-stage renal disease coverage are important, but raise distinctive issues that call for separate analysis.

All it takes to be automatically eligible for Medicare, if you are over age sixty-five, is eligibility for Social Security benefits. This, in turn, generally requires that either you or your spouse at some time worked during at least forty quarters (three-month periods). The spouse's death does not affect your eligibility, and you also can qualify, once past age sixty-five, as the dependent of a qualifying worker. In 2001, Medicare's senior enrollment numbered close to 35 million, a figure that is expected on demographic grounds to keep growing for many decades. By one recent estimate, Medicare reaches more than 98 percent of Americans over the age of sixty-five (Moon 1996, 241).

For reasons that are rooted in its history, Medicare offers two groupings of benefits—hospitalization insurance (HI) or Part A coverage, and supplementary medical insurance (SMI) or Part B coverage. This two-part structure is a residue of the political bidding process by which it was created in 1965. Part A was originally the Democratic plan to take a cautious first step, reflecting the lesson drawn from past political failure, toward comprehensive national healthcare for all Americans, not just seniors (Marmor 2000, 46). Part B started out as a Republican alternative, designed to offer a more market-like response (that is, voluntary and with insurance premiums) to seniors' healthcare needs. The Republicans' aim was to position themselves so that their opposition to the Democratic plan did not leave them looking like mere naysayers after Barry Goldwater's 1964 election debacle (Feingold 1966, 141–42). But their proposal ended up being co-opted as an add-on to the Democratic plan, although it kept vestigial traces of the underlying philosophical difference.

Part A Benefits

The principal Part A benefit is inpatient hospital care, and indeed everything else in Part A is essentially a spin-off of this coverage. Under the inpatient hospital care benefit, for each "spell of illness" you get up to sixty hospital days for free after paying an up-front deductible that in 2003 was $840. For days 61 through 90, you must pay coinsurance that in 2003 was $210 per day. With one exception, however, you then get no further Medicare coverage for inpatient hospital care until the next spell of illness, which requires a sixty-day break. The exception is that you have a one-time lifetime reserve of sixty extra days that you can tack on to any spell of illness, subject to paying coinsurance that in 2003 stood at $420 per day. There is no limit on the number of spells of illness that are covered.[1]

The second Part A benefit is skilled nursing facility (SNF) care. This generally must follow (within thirty days) a hospitalization of at least three days and be certified as medically necessary. You pay nothing for the first twenty days, and a daily copayment ($105 in 2003) for days 21 through 100. Medicare offers no SNF coverage past the hundredth day of a given post-hospitalization episode.

Part A also covers certain home health agency (HHA) care (such as nursing care) for a homebound beneficiary under a treatment plan directed by a doctor. Only part-time care is covered, but there is no time limit, and you pay no deductibles or copayments apart from a 20 percent share of the cost of certain medical supplies and equipment. In 1997, Congress transferred certain HHA benefits from Part A of Medicare to Part B. This served both to increase enrollee cost-sharing by the backdoor, and to permit the government to pretend that Medicare's financing had improved by the entire amount shifted.

Finally, Part A covers hospice care (such as pain relief, nursing services, and symptom management) for terminally ill people with life expectancies of six months or less who elect this care in lieu of the standard Medicare treatment of their illnesses. The patient makes only small copayments for drugs and inpatient respite care.

In compensating hospitals for providing Part A benefits, Medicare initially used cost-plus reimbursement, creating financial incentives for hospitals to run up the tab. In 1984, however, the Health Care Financing Administration (HCFA) that administered Medicare implemented a new Prospective Payment System (PPS) that aimed to make hospitals cost conscious. Under PPS, the patient's diagnosis at the time of admission generally determines what the hospital will get, and the hospital thus bears the difference between its expected and actual costs.

There is some evidence that PPS has succeeded in slowing the growth of Medicare's Part A costs (Dranove 2000, 52). One remaining problem, however, is that hospitals can boost their Medicare compensation by inflating their diagnoses of admitted patients (McClellan 1996, 149). This does not require anything reaching the level of conscious and outright fraud, given the ambiguity of many medical diagnoses.

Part B Benefits

In keeping with its 1965 Republican provenance, Part B coverage, which extends to most outpatient care, is voluntary and requires paying a premium. However, its terms are so favorable (since the premium pays only about a quarter of the costs) that one might call it a Don Corleone offer with a twist. It is an offer you almost cannot refuse, not because the consequences of refusal are so bad, but because those of acceptance are so good. Clearly, seniors see it this way, since nearly all enroll in Part B.

The coverage Part B offers for outpatient healthcare is so broad that it is easier to describe what it omits than what it covers.[2] The omission that long attracted the most attention was that for prescription drugs, although in mid-2003 this appeared to be on the verge of being addressed. Other omissions pertain to nursing and custodial care, dental care, eyeglasses, and hearing aids. Enrollees do, however, have to pay an annual $100 deductible, along with a monthly premium that in 2003 was $58.70 ($704.40 for the full year). In addition, for most Part B services, enrollees owe coinsurance equaling 20 percent of the Medicare-prescribed fee. For some services, the copayment is higher than this.

Doctors providing Part B services may have incentives to do more than is needed, but their compensation depends on the Medicare fee schedule rather than the costs they might claim to have incurred. The Center for Medicare and Medicaid Services, or CMS (HCFA's new name), compiles and periodically revises the Medicare fee schedule.

Healthcare Coverage That Medicare Does Not Offer

Among the items that Part B omits, several (such as dental care and eyeglasses) are relatively routine and predictable, and therefore in little need of insurance coverage against an unpredictable downside. However, the same cannot be said of prescription drugs (to the extent any newly enacted coverage remains incomplete) or nursing and custodial care, which may be unpredictably high for some individuals. These are widely recognized as serious gaps in Medicare, making its benefits package in some respects inferior to those offered by many employer-provided plans.

The other big gap in Medicare, however, relates not to a specific type of care, but to its placing no ceiling on the total amount that a beneficiary may have to pay. Many private health insurance plans have a "stop-loss" feature, under which the enrollee's maximum financial liability is capped at some dollar amount. Under Medicare, however, not only is Part A coverage time-limited, but Part B copayment liability, even at just 20 percent, can keep on climbing, for someone who needs a great deal of care, until it results in financial wipeout.

In 1988, Congress enacted legislation that added catastrophic coverage to Medicare, by loosening certain Part A restrictions and capping enrollees' Part B liability. Seniors as a group were to pay for the new coverage, in part through an income-related levy that was to be collected through the income tax. Within a year, however, massive popular resistance by well-organized seniors—most famously exemplified by a Monty Pythonesque riot, widely seen on television news shows, in which a group of seniors chased Congressman Rostenkowski down the street shouting such epithets as "Coward!" (Himelfarb 1995, 74)—led to its repeal. Among the main lessons drawn by many in the Washington policy community were that Medicare enrollees cannot be asked to pay more under any circumstances (see Graetz and Mashaw 1999, 270), and that catastrophic coverage is a "hard sell" to voters, notwithstanding its insurance value, "because, by definition, only a small proportion of enrollees will have occasion to use the benefits" (Moon 1996, 138).

No Topping Up

In both Part A and Part B, patients cannot "top up" their Medicare coverage by offering healthcare providers side payments in addition to the specified fee. In addition to reducing Medicare expenditures if some services or coverage are accordingly forgone, this may potentially benefit enrollees as a group. In effect, it organizes them as a cartel to offer healthcare providers nothing extra.

However, the no-topping-up rule also may prevent particular enrollees from getting more or better treatment that they would have been willing to pay for. This is not a mere side effect of the cartel, however (like a monopolist's lost sales if it cannot price discriminate). The ban on topping up reflects an underlying egalitarian norm with respect to healthcare treatment, by discouraging wealthy seniors from getting better healthcare than the rest through the requirement that the foot the entire bill themselves. More and more may begin choosing to do this, however, if doctors increasingly start dropping out of the program in response to tighter fee schedules.

Supplementary Medigap Coverage

Medicare enrollees who are concerned about gaps in their Medicare coverage, if willing and able to pay a market price for additional coverage, can do so via "Medigap" plans that a variety of private companies offer. Many of these plans offer missing Medicare benefits. For example, two-thirds of all Medicare enrollees have prescription drug coverage through their Medigap or other supplemental insurance (McClellan 2000b, 35), although the Medigap component of this coverage has been declining in apparent response to the rapid rise in prescription drug costs. Medigap plans also frequently cover Medicare's routine deductibles and copayments. The consequence may be that Medicare enrollees, having prepaid their expected out-of-pocket costs to the Medigap provider, retain no incentive to be cost conscious at the margin in selecting healthcare services (Bradford and Shaviro 2000, 46).

Suppose, for example, that a given senior is considering a relatively discretionary outpatient procedure that Medicare prices at $1,000. Absent Medigap coverage, the service would cost her a copayment of $200 (assuming exhaustion of Part B's $100 deductible). With the coverage, it costs her nothing, presumably increasing the chance that she will seek it even if she places a very low value on the medical benefit.

In pricing her Medigap coverage, the insurer will take into account the likelihood that the copayments the insured incurs will be affected by her not bearing them at the margin. The insurer will ignore, however, the fact that any increase in her use of healthcare also raises Medicare's costs by 80 percent of the extra tab. Thus, suppose it correctly guesses that she will consume an extra $1,000 in medical services (triggering an extra $200 copayment) due to Medigap's effect on her incentives, and therefore charges her an extra $200 for the coverage. Now it is happy because it has covered its costs, she is not too unhappy because at least she has eliminated the variance in her out-of-pocket costs, and the government (meaning taxpayers) is out $800.

No private insurer anywhere permits its customers to use side agreements that eliminate their cost consciousness to its uncompensated financial detriment. Yet, even though Medicare's Medigap problem is well known to policy analysts, and is estimated to have raised recent annual program expenditures by as much as $17 billion (Antos and Billheimer 1999, 27) or perhaps even $30 billion (Frech 1999, 113), nothing has yet been done. Presumably, those in responsible positions must consider the risk of being chased down the street by jeering mobs like poor Congressman Rostenkowski.

HMO Provisions

In the private healthcare market, unsupervised fee-for-service (FFS) arrangements are rapidly disappearing. They have been replaced by managed care, such as through health maintenance organizations (HMOs) that limit authorized providers to a practice group and require a primary care physician (PCP) to approve referrals to specialists. The PCP, in turn, typically has financial incentives not to approve unlimited care.

A key rationale for the introduction of managed care was that it could operate on the supply side to tamp down exploding healthcare costs. In particular, it tries to address doctors' incentives to engage in "demand inducement," or the exploitation of diagnostic ambiguity and patients' lack of medical expertise to recommend unneeded or non-cost-effective treatment (Aaron 1991, 15). However, the actual cost savings are disputed in the literature. One recent estimate placed them at over $300 billion annually (Dranove 2000, 3). More recently, confidence about the cost saving has been declining, due in part to the legal, political, and consumer pressures that increasingly discourage insurers from tightening the screws. In any event, largely for technological reasons, overall healthcare costs have continued to rise not only in real terms, but relative to the size of the economy (45).

Many Medicare reformers, noticing the private-sector shift to managed care, have been eager to capture similar cost savings for the government (along with any quality advantages of managed care to interested enrollees). As early as 1982, Congress amended the Medicare rules to permit HMO participation in the program, and it has continued to tinker with these rules. There have, however, been two persistent problems. The first one is that, while Medicare's HMO sector for a time grew rapidly, it has remained comparatively small, covering (as of 2002) less than 16 percent of enrollees. The bigger problem, however, is that, due to poor design, Medicare's HMO rules appear over time to have actually cost, rather than saved, the government money (Reischauer 2000, 415).

Under what is now called "Medicare + Choice," enrollees can choose an officially approved HMO or other managed care plan that offers all Medicare services. The HMO may charge a premium in lieu of the Part A and Part B deductibles and coinsurance amounts, and may also offer additional services, such as prescription drug coverage or the use of health-club facilities. Medicare compensates the HMO by paying it, for each enrollee, 95 percent of the average benefit payments for what it deems to be a similar individual in traditional FFS Medicare. If, however, the HMO makes higher profits from Medicare than in its private business, it must either rebate the extra cash to the government or use it to give enrollees greater benefits—the HMO's preferred course, since this helps attract more customers from whom an ordinary profit can be made, rather than being a complete loss to it.

Right from the start, therefore, Medicare's potential cost saving from HMOs is limited. What has made the fiscal impact actually negative over time, however, is the fact that Medicare HMOs have been able to attract enrollees who offer better-than-average health risks, and who thus would have cost Medicare less than its payments to the participating HMOs.[3] This partly reflects the fact that HMOs' potential service rationing function inherently makes them more appealing to healthier individuals (all else equal). It also may reflect deliberate marketing strategies by HMOs that understand how they may gain by disproportionately attracting the healthy through the extra benefits they choose to provide. An example would be offering healthclub facilities that are only valued by people who are fit enough for vigorous exercise.

Congress tried to address this biased selection problem in 1997 by instructing the CMS to implement better risk-adjusting of the amounts it pays HMOs, beginning in 2000. The success of these efforts is at yet unknown. However, there is already disturbing evidence that many HMOs, perhaps concerned about possible undercompensation under the adjusted formulas, are responding by terminating their Medicare contracts or reducing their service areas (Reischauer 2000, 424).

Why wouldn't Medicare + Choice permit cash rebates to customers rather than just extra services that they may value below cost? Or why not permit HMOs to keep part of their extra profits while rebating the rest, thus compensating them more if they save the government money? A part of the answer may be Soviet-style concern about exposing FFS inefficiencies to direct public view, or allowing the appearance of "profiteering" at the government's expense even if everyone comes out ahead. In addition, however, something more principled and defensible may have been involved. The sheer waste that results if an HMO dissipates its extra profits through benefits that its enrollees value at below cost does at least dampen the incentive to put even greater efforts into biased selection. Such efforts might end up costing the government even more money if it did not risk-adjust well enough.

Related Government Programs to Supply Health Insurance

Medicare is only one of the federal government's three big interventions to provide health insurance coverage. The other two, Medicaid and the provision of tax subsidies for employer-provided health insurance, are worth briefly considering due to the interaction between their benefits and those provided by Medicare.

Medicaid

In 1965, Congress enacted not only Medicare to serve the elderly, but also Medicaid to serve favored groups among the poor, such as households with dependent children and also certain seniors. Medicaid provides full payment for the covered medical expenses of beneficiaries, who generally must meet income and asset tests that are designed to limit the program to the poor and near-poor. The program has grown to the point that, in 2000, it spent $207 billion (split between the federal government and the states) in serving 41.7 million beneficiaries. This leaves it slightly smaller than Medicare, measured by expenditures, although it serves about 6 million more people. Medicaid's lower per capita expenditure partly reflects its covering what is on average a healthier population, along with the fact that, when both programs would cover a given service, Medicare pays the bill. In addition, Medicaid often provides lower payments to service providers than does Medicare, with the consequence that fewer providers accept it. But on the other hand, Medicaid often provides certain benefits that Medicare generally does not. Examples include prescription drug coverage, nursing home care past the one-hundred-day Medicare limit, and the cost of such items as hearing aids and eyeglasses.

The fact that Medicare enrollees can also qualify for Medicaid benefits has two main practical implications. First, enrollees whose incomes are below the poverty line and who have less than $6,000 of assets (for married couples, and excluding certain items such as homes and household goods) have all of their Medicare premiums and cost-sharing charges paid by Medicaid. Those sufficiently near the poverty line have their Part B premiums paid by Medicaid, thus helping to ensure that they will elect Part B coverage. Second, seniors who qualify for Medicaid can use it to fill in the gaps in Medicare coverage, such as for prescription drugs and long-term nursing care. In a typical scenario, an individual who needs long-term nursing home care might first use Medicare, then spend down her assets to the requisite poverty level, and then start getting Medicaid coverage.

Income and Payroll Tax Subsidies for Employer-Provided Health Insurance

The government's second big health insurance intervention outside Medicare involves the design of federal and state income taxes, along with the payroll taxes that fund Social Security and Medicare. All of these taxes generally exclude from taxable income or compensation the value of employer-provided health insurance. The estimated revenue cost in 2003, just for the federal income tax exclusion, was $79.6 billion (Joint Committee on Taxation 2002, 28). The other exclusions raise the annual revenue cost to more than $100 billion per year (Shiels and Hogan 1999, 179).

The value of these exclusions varies with individuals' marginal tax rates. According to a recent estimate, however, they lower the median after-tax price of employer-provided health insurance by more than one-third (Gruber and Lettau 2000, 31).[4] Thus, the median worker and her employer may mutually benefit from substituting health insurance for cash wages in her compensation package, right up to the point where the last dollar of coverage offers benefits that she values at roughly 65 cents.

One of the key incentive effects of this tax wedge is encouraging more workers to have health insurance. A second is encouraging those who would insure anyway to choose more comprehensive plans—extending, for example, to routine and predictable medical expenses that really do not need to be insured. In effect, medical expenses become fully deductible under the income and payroll taxes,[5] but subject to having the insurance company cover them as they arise. Unfortunately, this may induce wasteful overexpenditure, since if the insurance company is on the hook then the consumer does not bear the marginal cost of extra treatment. While consumers in the aggregate pay for the waste through higher premiums, they nonetheless individually gain from their own waste until it reaches the point of exceeding the tax benefit.

The tax incentive for workers to overinsure may have a spillover effect on Medicare's coverage. By reducing a large group of consumers' cost consciousness at the margin, it may increase both prices and treatment norms in the entire healthcare sector. It also encourages workers (and thus voters) to think that healthcare benefits can be provided for free (see Pauly 1999a, 95). Moreover, it tends to direct medical research toward procedures that will be profitable when marketed to non-cost-conscious consumers. The consumer incentive problems inherent to Medicare itself are accentuated rather than counteracted by the existence of parallel, if not quite so capacious, limits on cost consciousness elsewhere.

The Financing Side of Medicare

Payroll Tax Financing for Part A Coverage
Part A of Medicare, like Social Security, is officially financed by a slice of the federal payroll tax on people's earnings. Overall, this tax applies at a 14.2 percent effective rate on earnings up to an annual ceiling that, for 2003, effectively though not officially stood at $93,655 (see Shaviro 2000a, 10–11),[6] and at a flat 2.9 percent rate on earnings above the ceiling.[7] Nominally, workers and employers each pay half, with the employer's share being excluded from the income and payroll tax bases. Economists agree, however, that the incidence of the payroll tax—that is, who really bears it given how wages would adjust if it were eliminated—

is largely unaffected by this nominal split (Rosen 1999, 189). The officially designated Medicare slice (the rest being attributed to Social Security) is 2.9 percent both below and above the annual ceiling. In 2001, this share of the payroll tax raised $151.9 billion, or 63 percent of Medicare's $240.9 billion in total outlays for the year.

Why use a specified portion of the payroll tax, rather than general revenues, to pay for a portion of Medicare? The main reason is that Medicare's 1965 Democratic sponsors wanted "to provide universal coverage as an earned benefit, rather than as a charity payment, to all those who had contributed during their working lives" (Marmor 2000, 137). Indeed, they felt strongly enough to make this "peculiar choice" (Oberlander 2003, 137) of financing tool even though the payroll tax (which at the time was capped at $6,600 of annual earnings) was far less progressive than the income tax.[8]

For at least one leading Medicare sponsor—Ways and Means Chairman Wilbur Mills—payroll tax financing was a sword against benefit expansion as well as a shield against curtailment. Mill considered it a mechanism for protecting the fisc against the risk that Part A would prove to be costlier than expected (Patashnik and Zelizer 2001, 18–20). But Mills might have had a harder time winning acceptance of the "sword" if not for the more widely understood "shield" aspect of dedicated financing.

Premiums and General Revenue Financing for Part B Coverage

The Republican proponents of what became Part B were averse to creating an open-ended, Social Security-like entitlement with earmarked financing. Having in mind something more akin to subsidized private health insurance, they proposed instead to charge enrollees premiums, while using general revenues to augment the value of the coverage. The premiums they proposed would have been pegged to the level of enrollees' Social Security benefits, thus ensuring that people with higher lifetime earnings generally would pay more (Marmor 2000, 48).

The Democrats, upon incorporating this plan into their own Medicare package, made the premiums uniform rather than scaled to Social Security earnings. As in Part A, the idea seems to have been that sacrificing some of the progressivity was worth it if the benefits thereby looked more "earned" and hence inviolable. So once again the Democrats sacrificed progressivity in order to strengthen the "shield" (and perhaps for a few, such as Mills, the "sword") aspect of the program's financing.

The premiums are set by law under a formula that is designed to peg them at about 25 percent of Part B program costs. Initially, the percentage was 50 percent, but Congress in 1972 responded to rapidly rising Part B costs, which adversely affected both enrollees and taxpayers, by reducing enrollees' share. It thereby, in the long run, handed taxpayers a double whammy with respect to the cost escalation. In 2001, revenue from the premiums totaled $22.3 billion, or about 9 percent of overall Medicare expenditure.

The Medicare Trust Funds

When Congress created Medicare in 1965, it established a set of accounting procedures to help keep track of the relationship over time between the program's expenditures and revenues. For Part A, the objective of using a slice of the payroll tax to finance benefits required tracking the designated revenues against expenditures over the life of the program, since they were not going to be equalized on a cash-flow basis each year. Even for Part B, it made sense to chart the path of expenditures and consequent revenue needs, given the intention to create a secure entitlement.

So far so good; but unfortunately, taking a page from Social Security, Congress named the accounts that would be tracking Medicare revenues and expenditures the Part A and Part B "trust funds." It thereby guaranteed that these accounts' real significance would be widely misunderstood. We normally think of trust funds as actually paying for things. Twenty-year-olds with trust funds, for example, are more often found buying sports cars or vacationing in Europe than working at Burger King, because they can draw on the savings that some ancestor has set aside for them. A bank or insurance company might be holding these funds, with legally binding instructions regarding how and when to dole them out.

The Medicare trust funds are quite different. They neither hold actual assets, nor reflect the setting aside of funds, nor create a binding legal obligation to pay anyone, including Medicare enrollees, anything. (Any such obligations result only from laws on the books that Congress can change at any time.) They are merely a set of notes that the government keeps regarding how, under specified conventions, the intended funding for the program is shaping up. These notes provide a historical record of cash flows occurring either between the government and third parties and officially attributed to Medicare, or else deemed to have occurred within the government. The trust fund balances could therefore be changed at any time—for example, by Congress's announcing a trillion-dollar "deposit" in the Part A Trust Fund—without improving, or even necessarily affecting, the actual financing of Medicare or any other government program.

The Part A Trust Fund does, concededly, have legal significance under present law, since, if it were exhausted, Part A benefit payments would have to be limited to current payroll tax receipts until Congress took action of some kind. (The Part B Trust Fund, by contrast, can virtually be ignored since it automatically gets the general revenues needed to meet its costs.) This is unlikely to happen, however, given Congress's power to restore the positive balance of the Part A Trust Fund by simple declaration or to waive the positive-balance requirement.

Even though exhaustion of the Part A Trust Fund is unlikely to be permitted, its approach may have significant political effects. Up to now, the usual response has been to increase dedicated payroll taxes rather than to cut benefits. However, if a payroll tax increase has sufficiently high political costs, then the idea of Wilbur Mills to constrain benefit growth by tying it, through the Trust Fund, to a specific financing mechanism might conceivably bear fruit.

Many people, including members of Congress, may interpret the Trust Fund idea quite differently than this. One sometimes discerns the view, reminiscent of Clown family accounting, that we can actually pay for Medicare by mere declaration regarding the Part A Trust Fund. An example was the 1997 legislation shifting most home healthcare costs to Part B. This officially extended the program's period of expected solvency by six years. Yet, if this shift mattered at all, other than through its substantive effect on copayments, it actually made things worse by reducing the perceived pressure to address Medicare's financing problems (Kahn 1998, 53).

Along the same lines, consider 1993 legislation that boosted the Part A Trust Fund by providing that the revenues from a newly enacted increase in the income taxation of people's Social Security benefits would be contributed to it.[9] Congress actually did address the overall fiscal gap enacting this tax increase (assuming its other taxing and spending decisions were unaffected). The decision to "contribute" the proceeds to Part A of Medicare, however, had no direct significance. The Treasury evidences this "contribution" by making annual deposits in the Part A Trust Fund that, for 2001, equaled about $4.9 billion. Alas, however, we cannot actually pay for things by writing checks to ourselves.

If the "contribution" mattered at all, it was indirectly, by affecting congressional decisions that were based on the premise that the stated Part A Trust Fund balance is significant. Similarly, anything in the world matters if enough people act as if it does—be it the convention that gold is valuable because everyone else values it, or the tenets of astrology if people follow what they believe to be its counsel.

In 1993, Congress might not have agreed to increase the income taxation of Social Security benefits unless the extra revenues were being credited to Medicare. Subsequently, the attribution may have reduced Congress's proclivity at the margin to enact tax cuts or spending increases outside of Medicare. The attribution may encourage viewing the revenues as having been placed in a conceptual "lockbox," and thus as unavailable for other uses. A similar argument would hold that the practice of excluding Social Security's current cash-flow surplus from the officially reported "on-budget" surplus or deficit makes Congress more fiscally prudent, because it regards that measure as significant. Only, in the case of Medicare, this result is hoped for without removing Part A from the official on-budget measure.

There are two diametrically opposed reasons why this "lockbox" argument about Part A might be incorrect. One is that only the official on-budget measure affects Congress's current tax and spending decisions, since this measure is so prominent in public debate. So any annual Part A surplus would need to be excluded from the official budget measure before any perceptual benefits would result. The opposite, but (in this regard) equally discouraging possibility, is that Congress actually looks at the broader fiscal picture. It might primarily heed the "unified" budget surplus or deficit, or in the alternative pay no significant attention to labeling issues of this kind.

Even if the Medicare trust funds are in some respects a useful accounting convention, one must remember that they do not actually provide financing. If we respond to long-term financing concerns by simply padding the Part A Trust Fund, we will still have to deal with that imbalance in the long run, only with less advance warning and fewer options. And if we choose a particular financing response, such as a payroll tax increase or Part A benefit cut, simply because we are fixated on the imbalance in the Trust Fund, we may miss the opportunity to ask more fundamentally how we want to share benefits and burdens among our citizens.

Summary

On the spending side, Medicare's coverage for both Part A hospital care and Part B outpatient care is substantial and generous, yet flawed on both the low end, concerning routine coverage, and the high end, concerning catastrophic and long-term coverage. On the low end, once enrollees have purchased Medigap coverage, they may have no incentive to be cost conscious with respect to routine expenditures. No private insurer would similarly permit its customers to use side agreements to wipe out their cost-sharing, to its uncompensated financial detriment. Medicare's excursions into managed care, the main private-sector vehicle for trying to increase cost consciousness, have actually cost it money due to questionable design. On the high end, Medicare enrollees lack catastrophic coverage, and thus can only look to Medicaid (once they have depleted their assets) if their medical needs outstrip their means. Medicare therefore provides both too little insurance coverage and too much, if the aim of insurance is to reduce the variability of unpredictable expenditure needs.

On the financing side, Medicare's design is not as clearly flawed. One historically interesting point, however, concerns its use of two key financing tools that are less progressive than the federal income tax: the payroll tax for Part A, and what is in effect a uniform head tax to pay for one-quarter of Part B. Both were chosen by Medicare's Democratic proponents, in lieu of more progressive financing tools that Republicans proposed, so that Medicare would look more like an "earned benefit" rather than a "charity payment."

The earmarking that the Democrats chose for Part A, while literally just an accounting convention, may actually affect outcomes up to a point. It may serve as both a sword against benefit expansion and a shield against benefit curtailment. Yet the ability to play games with mere bookkeeping measures, or to confuse them with an underlying substance that they lack, should caution us against holding out too much hope that they will be effective.

The idea of financing Medicare Part A through a dedicated portion of the payroll tax logically entails keeping some set of accounts, such as those underlying the Part A Trust Fund. However, the Trust Fund's significance should not be misunderstood. Merely a kind of historical record computed under particular assumptions, it cannot actually pay for Medicare in the sense that dinner ingredients come out of the pantry. Viewing the Part A Trust Fund as an actual financing source, and thus believing that we can finance Medicare just by adding to the amounts officially attributed to it, is akin to believing that you can pay for your children's college education by depositing self-owed IOUs in a desk drawer.

Medicare's Incentive and Distributional Effects

The Frequent Trade-Off between Incentives and Distribution

THE Medicare benefit and financing rules that we examined in chapter 2 are important due to their incentive and distributional effects. That is, they matter because they affect both efficiency (and thus the size of the economic pie) and distribution (or how people divide the pie).

As a broad generalization, what we are usually trying to do with a fiscal system such as Medicare is improve distribution at a tolerable efficiency cost. To illustrate the typical trade-off between efficiency and distribution, consider the income tax as well as income-related transfer systems such as welfare and Food Stamps. Under these systems, the more you earn, the more you pay or the less you get. Thus, they penalize work and saving. By contrast, if we had a uniform head tax and no income-conditioned transfer systems, work and saving would be neither punished nor rewarded (leaving aside the question of how we would actually collect the tax from people too poor to pay it).

If we thought only about incentives, it is hard to see why we would want to penalize work and saving by having income-conditioned fiscal rules instead of a uniform head tax. Yet few would on balance favor eliminating these penalties through the creation of a system under which Bill Gates would pay the same tax as a homeless person and no one would get a transfer, no matter how dire her circumstances and how little she could have avoided them.

Likewise, if we thought only about distribution, there would be an argument for total wealth equalization in the society, or else for following Marx's credo, "From each according to his abilities, to each according to his needs." Either of these approaches, however, would virtually eliminate incentives to work and save, since people's efforts would no longer influence what they ended up with. The result might be a collapse of productive effort in the society.

Accordingly, in examining Medicare's incentive and distributional effects, we should retain a proper sense of perspective about each. Incentive effects, up to a point, can be adverse without undue concern so long as the distributional gain exceeds the efficiency loss. Bad distributional effects might merit more immediate criticism, however, since they would raise the possibility of a lose–lose interaction whereby social waste is the by-product of transferring resources to people who need them less than the transferors.

Incentives under the Current System

Seniors

Medicare's most dramatic incentive effect is on its enrollees' inclination to seek healthcare. For example, under Part B, an enrollee might rationally choose to undergo a $100 procedure even if its subjective value to her was only $20. With Medigap coverage of her Medicare copayments, she might choose to undergo the procedure even if its value to her was close to zero. Part A similarly induces zero cost consciousness once you have used up your deductibles (or even from the first dollar under some Medigap plans), until the point where the coverage runs out.

Suppose that I pay $20, and the government through Medicare pays $80, for a medical service that I value at exactly $30. Ordinarily, or in the absence of broader considerations that we will see are quite important in the Medicare setting, this would be a classic case of inefficiency. Economists define inefficiency in terms of deadweight loss, or waste in the sense that one person's loss is not offset by anyone else's gain, thus leaving society as a whole the poorer. In this instance, if the government had simply given me $80 and I had decided to keep the money, I would apparently have been $70 better off than in the actual state of affairs. After all, I would have ended up with an extra $100 of cash (including my own $20) while being out only $30 in terms of the subjective value of services forgone. To the taxpayers, by contrast, the cost of giving me cash instead of Medicare benefits would have been exactly the same.

So Medicare would seemingly have resulted in wasting $70, although the nature of the waste may be counterintuitive. Even though I remain the overall winner in this story, it is I—not the taxpayers—who has lost $70 relative to the counterfactual state of affairs that may conveniently help measure the inefficiency.[1] After all, they would still be out $80 if I valued the medical service at its full cost. And any amount by which they do benefit me is a transfer with a winner as well as a loser, not an instance of deadweight loss.

In describing such an inefficiency, we should keep in mind that its measure depends on how much I would have paid for the healthcare if given the taxpayers' $80 with no strings attached—*not* on how much I would have paid for it if given nothing. No waste is involved if I simply start spending more because I have more money to spend. That would be an example of what economists call an "income effect," well-illustrated by Michael Jordan's willingness, upon his second retirement (in 1998), implicitly to pay $30 million for a year of leisure by turning down that salary for one more season as a basketball player. Surely he would not have been willing to pay so much for the leisure had he not already been so rich. Similarly, through income effects, Medicare may increase healthcare spending without evidencing inefficiency. After all, if people can newly afford medical treatment that they desperately want, that does not indicate that they would have preferred to spend the money on something else.

Suppose, however, that Medicare contributes $80 toward the cost of a $100 healthcare service for which I would have paid only $30 if offered $80 in cash with no strings attached. Even now, as I discuss in chapter 5, this may not be inefficient after all. For example, I might be mistaken regarding the healthcare's benefit to me. Or the taxpayers might benefit, in one way or another, from giving me healthcare instead of cash that I would have preferred. Still, if Medicare is indeed giving people healthcare services that they value at below the total cost, then we have an issue of possible inefficiency.

Despite the enormous wedge that Medicare drives between the social cost of healthcare services and their cost to the enrollee, waste does not automatically result even if we only count the enrollees' revealed preferences. The amount of waste depends on what economists call the "income-compensated elasticity of demand" for medical services. That is, how price sensitive are people in seeking healthcare when they have the cash to pay for it? It is natural to intuit that people will *not* be very price sensitive (and thus that offering cash would not greatly change their decisions). After all, if you are in pain you probably want relief, and if your health is endangered you may be eager to get the best treatment possible. As the saying goes, life and health are priceless (meaning really that other available goods cannot compensate for their absence).

This intuition is very likely true up to a point. For example, it is plausible that an 80 percent or 100 percent income tax would discourage work effort far more than Medicare encourages extra medical expenditure. Not only is being healthy typically a high priority, but many of the key decisions are made by doctors. Their incentives, while requiring separate consideration below, generally do not include a direct stake in the patient's out-of-pocket costs. Moreover, while some patients may shop around until they find a doctor who they believe will offer the care they want and no other care, others are more passive.

Nonetheless, people's preferences, at a given income level, for medical treatment are not entirely fixed. For one thing, the medical treatment you seek is subject to substantial modification depending on your preferences. Rather than just involving yes or no decisions on such matters as whether to unblock a key artery through open heart surgery, it frequently involves patient choice up and down the line. We might start with lifestyle choices that affect health, and then move on to decisions about whether to see a doctor when one begins to feel uncomfortable or to have a health concern. Even after deciding to see a doctor, patients may have numerous choices to make between doctors, medical tests that are judgment calls, varying treatment options, and the like. The fact that many of us do not make healthcare decisions very price-consciously reflects the fact that both Medicare and employer-provided health insurance typically foot most of the bill anyway.

The revenue estimates suggesting that Medigap coverage of copayments annually costs Medicare $17 billion (Antos and Billheimer 1999, 27) to $30 billion (Frech 1999, 113) provide initial evidence of price responsiveness. These estimates are based on detailed empirical studies of Medicare enrollees' spending patterns. Contamination by income effects is limited, since Medigap insurers charge people for the expected level of their Medicare copayments.[2]

More broadly, general cost consciousness in healthcare was reliably documented in the 1970s in what is known as the "RAND study." This study, "one of the largest and longest-running social science research projects ever completed" (Newhouse et al. 1993, vii), "generated widely accepted estimates of the magnitude" of patients' responsiveness to cost sharing, and strongly influenced plan design by insurers with real monetary stakes in understanding the healthcare market (Dranove 2000, 30–31). In the RAND study, several thousand individuals were randomly assigned to one of five insurance plans that ranged from providing healthcare for free to requiring patients to pay as much as 95 percent of their annual healthcare costs up to a $1,000 ceiling. (The ceiling helped limit income effects on expenditure.) The study found that "cost sharing markedly decreases use of all types of services among all types of people," with an annual per-person expenditure reduction of about 30 percent under the 95 percent copayment plan as compared to the free plan (Newhouse et al. 1993, 79). Moreover, it found that "reduced service use under the cost-sharing plans had little or no net adverse effect on health for the average person"—although with the important caveat that the sick poor, who often might be covered by Medicaid, *were* adversely affected (339).

The RAND study was limited to a nonelderly population. There is reason to believe, however, that (controlling for income) elderly patients are likely to be, if anything, more price responsive than younger ones. Sherry Glied (1997, 78) notes the importance, in deterring overuse of healthcare services, of "[t]he non-monetary, noninsurable costs—pain, suffering, and time—associated with becoming ill and using many medical services." And while it would be hard to say how pain sensitive we are when old compared to when young (although surely pain becomes more of a daily companion), it is clear enough that retirees, whose children if any are likely to be grown, tend to have more free time than workers and the parents of young children. So in one key respect at least, their implicit, non-monetary copayments are lower, potentially making the financial costs a greater relative influence on their decisions.

It thus appears clear that Medicare's cost sharing (or lack thereof) affects not just enrollees' abstract incentives but their real-world behavior. The implication is that they may often choose services that are worth less to them than the social cost, suggesting straight inefficiency unless the gap can be rationalized on other grounds as consistent with good social policy.

Healthcare Providers

The healthcare industry has multiple players whose incentives may in some respects diverge. All are influenced by a fundamental incentive problem that any healthcare system, whether government-dominated or mainly private, must confront in some fashion. Doctors typically perform the dual functions of diagnosis and treatment. What they say in the former capacity may therefore affect what they earn in the latter capacity. Moreover, the diagnoses that they are called on to make are often quite ambiguous. And even when the proper diagnosis is relatively clearcut, doctors understand that they generally are dealing with lay patients whose medical expertise is far inferior to their own.

Healthcare is therefore liable to involve the same unfortunate incentives and opportunities that have made automobile repair mechanics the objects of such widespread suspicion. And healthcare involves considerably higher stakes than automobile repair, not just financially but in terms of the importance of good care. Fortunately, doctors' inclination to use good faith in performing their dual function may be enhanced by a deeply rooted ideology of patient service, embodied in the norms of medical ethics that each doctor voices upon taking the Hippocratic Oath. What is more, while doctors are well paid, the training they undergo is sufficiently long and arduous, even compared to that in the other licensed professions, that medicine may tend disproportionately to attract people who value the end result of helping and healing people. In effect, medicine offers such individuals higher pay (in the form of job satisfaction) than it offers those who are indifferent to this end.

Nonetheless, when doctors make or strongly influence healthcare decisions that affect their own financial well-being, the problem of agency cost rears its well-manicured head. And when doctors or hospital administrators know that by doing more they can earn more, the agency cost problem takes the form of demand inducement, or encouraging the provision of excessive medical services.

At least in a pre–managed care world, the empirical importance of demand inducement has been documented (as in Fuchs 1978). It has the potential to encourage not merely healthcare that is worth less than it costs, but that would be against the patient's best interests even at a monetary cost of zero. Treatment can have its own risks and nonmonetary costs, such as pain and lost time, in addition to its benefits. And overtreatment may remain a significant problem today even insofar as managed care has addressed demand inducement. Concern about legal liability may induce doctors to practice "defensive medicine," such as by administering unneeded tests that offer the patient too little benefit to be worth the nonmonetary costs.

Once we combine demand inducement with limited cost consciousness, the dynamic consequences for the evolution of healthcare can be quite powerful. For example, economists have documented a "medical arms race" between hospitals, which compete to provide top-of-the-line treatment (in terms of both staffing and technology) that raises costs to third-party payers yet may actually worsen care. Once everyone is offering the same specialized service (such as high-tech cardiac treatment), no one gets to develop as much experience as quickly in administering it. Because experience is often crucial to quality (Luft et al. 1990), more robust competition may perversely end up making treatment worse rather than better.

Similarly, it is not a law of nature that advances in medical technology must increase healthcare costs. Innovations may be cost-saving, not just more powerful, and improved medications or techniques for early diagnosis may help to forestall costly illness. As Burton Weisbrod (1991) first noted, the actual history of inexorably increasing costs may reflect the incentives faced by medical research and development firms. Unlike the firms in most industries, they have operated with the understanding that they could more easily make money by increasing quality than by reducing cost (Dranove 2000, 46).

Again, these fundamental incentive problems crop up not just for Medicare but throughout the healthcare sector of the economy, particularly once we have strong tax incentives for pervasive overinsurance of routine expenses. Staggering recent increases in prescription drug costs (Pear 2001) may reflect incentive problems in the healthcare industry, albeit not from Medicare given the gap in its coverage. Medicare does, however, in some respects face worse incentive problems than the private insurance sector given the continuing prevalence under Part B of fee-for-service arrangements.

On the Part A hospital care front, Medicare has done somewhat better than in Part B, through the adoption of Prospective Payment System (PPS) rules that give hospitals an incentive to economize once they have admitted a patient with a given diagnosis. Even here, however, such cost control as has resulted (notwithstanding hospitals' incentive to inflate the diagnoses on admission) is increasingly threatened. In the view of some commentators, the growing practice of carving out portions of the inpatient treatment package to be billed to Medicare separately has brought the system's pricing structure close to the point of collapse (Newhouse 2001). This practice responds to the fact that Medicare's payment for a given hospitalization may stay the same even if items that previously were part of the hospitalization package begin to be charged to it as separate items.

Workers and Savers

The need to pay for Medicare through taxes that bear some relationship to ability to pay leads to a further set of incentive effects. Income and payroll taxes reduce people's incentive to work, and income taxes additionally reduce their incentive to save.[3] In addition, because both tax bases exclude various employee fringe benefits, such as employer-provided health insurance, they induce using these items in compensation agreements, even if the employee values them at below the employer's cost.

There are two main reasons why these work and saving disincentives might be a concern. The first is the standard deadweight loss problem that we earlier considered with regard to healthcare expenditure. Suppose I would be willing to mow a homeowner's lawn so long as I was paid at least $40, and that she was willing to pay me up to $50 to do it. My doing the job would create $10 of social surplus—the excess of a mowed lawn's value to her over the disvalue to me of doing the job. (Where the wage landed between $40 and $50 would determine how we split the surplus.) However, a wage or income tax on me of greater than 20 percent would prevent us from reaching a mutually advantageous agreement, and thus destroy this surplus.

Second, people's work and saving may have positive externalities. They may boost the society's capital stock, permitting future generations to enjoy higher standards of living. In addition, by boosting the capital stock, they may have desirable future distributional effects, such as from increasing productivity and thus wages at the low end, as well as offering a return to capital at the high end.

The significance of these problems in the Medicare context is reasonably debatable. Medicare uses a dedicated payroll tax rate of 2.9 percent, plus nearly 6 percent of the income tax in current cash flow terms. This makes it just one contributor among many to the overall tax wedges with regard to the returns from work and saving, albeit no trivial contributor. Moreover, the tax responsiveness of both work and saving to changes in incentives at the margin is much disputed in the economics literature and, according to some plausible estimates, is fairly low.

A more serious concern about Medicare, from the standpoint of the capital stock, relates to its effect on saving when younger generations pay for older generations' retirement healthcare. This may tend to reduce the older generations' saving due to an income effect. People may ask themselves: "Why save for my own retirement healthcare if someone else—as yet unborn, and thus not saving yet—is going to pay for it?"

Distributional Effects of the Current System

Medicare's dominant purpose is distributional. It is supposed to ensure adequate healthcare to people who might otherwise go untreated. This purpose, however, looks only to the benefit side. Medicare's overall distributional effects depend not just on what people get, but on the relationship between what they get and what they have paid.

Given the program's basic design as retirement health insurance financed by payroll and income taxes, one might expect that it would have two main distributional effects. The first is transfers from the rich to the poor, since high-earners end up paying the most for uniform coverage. The second is transfers from the healthy to the sick, since the latter might be expected to make greater use of their health insurance coverage. However, the actual transfer picture in Medicare is considerably more complicated.

Intergenerational

Medicare's most notable distributional feature has been its wealth transfer from younger to older generations. This has resulted not from its steady-state design, but from its enactment and steady growth. People born in 1900 began to receive benefits after 1965 even though (assuming retirement at that point) they had paid no Medicare taxes. Those born in the ensuing thirty to forty years received larger transfers still, as their payment of some Medicare taxes was more than offset by the growth in Medicare spending. By the time we get to people born in 1960, however, Medicare projects to be a losing proposition even if we (1) conservatively assume that they would only need a 3 percent return on their tax contributions to break even, and (2) ignore the likelihood of substantial adverse changes to the system's current tax and benefit rules (Cutler and Sheiner 2000, 304).[4]

Medicare's generational transfers are quite significant. For example, under current policy, people born in 1920 or 1930 in effect "receive about $50,000 net per person reaching age 65 in 2000 dollars" (304). Those born in 1980 and thereafter may well face losses that are considerably larger than this, depending on how the program performs over time and what steps are taken to restore its long-term sustainability. Making the transfers more significant still is the fact that, as I discuss in chapter 7, the rest of the fiscal system accentuates, rather than offsets, them.

Within Age Cohorts

Within age cohorts, Medicare has a number of distributional effects, including those between high- and low-earners, singles versus marrieds, people with different health conditions and needs, and those living in different parts of the country.

Progressivity. If just one assumption about Medicare's distributional effects would seem to be safe, it would be that the system results in substantial progressive redistribution, or transfers from people who on a lifetime basis are high-earners to those who are low-earners. After all, everyone gets the same insurance coverage upon retirement, but during your working years you pay a flat rate tax, with the result that high-earners pay more.

This assumption about Medicare's progressivity appears to be mistaken, due to a phenomenon that brings to mind the old witticism that the law, in its impartial majesty, forbids rich and poor alike to sleep under bridges. Here the point is that, while the rich sleep under bridges less than the poor, they use healthcare more. Thus, giving both groups the same set of rights to subsidized healthcare results in Medicare usage patterns that are positively correlated with lifetime income (McClellan and Skinner 1997, 6).

What could explain this correlation, which seems in tension with the fact that poor health is more endemic among the poor? The main explanations include the following:

• For a given healthcare problem, higher-income individuals tend to demand more healthcare services and greater treatment intensity (25). While this may partly reflect income-related barriers to seeking treatment, the pattern is also found in countries such as England that offer free national healthcare to all citizens (LeGrand 1982, 26). The reasons for it are not entirely known, but are likely to include income-related differences in medical information and/or consumer preferences. In addition, lifetime income, to the extent correlated with something observable, may influence what treatment doctors recommend for a given individual.

• Higher-income individuals tend to live longer, and thus to receive their generally more intensive care for a longer time period (McClellan and Skinner 1997, 7). This apparently outweighs the fact that, by dying later, they defer the generally most intensive period of expenditure, which is near the end of one's life (24).[5]

• Due to income effects, richer individuals may be more willing than poorer ones to bear a given out-of-pocket cost of Medicare coverage. In addition, people at higher income levels tend to hold more Medigap coverage (23), thus increasing their incentives at the margin to seek Medicare-subsidized services.

• Higher-income people tend to live in cities, where medical costs, along with treatment intensity and availability, are generally higher than in rural areas (22–23).

In combination, these factors create so pronounced a correlation between lifetime income and Medicare usage that a 1997 study by Mark McClellan and Jonathan Skinner, using data through 1990, found "a net flow of benefits from low-income to higher-income individuals that have reached Medicare eligibility to date." McClellan and Skinner found, moreover, that Medicare's net benefit flow would continue indefinitely to travel in this direction except that, in the future, the very lowest income groups would win and the very highest would lose (47).[6]

More recent data have made this conclusion less certain. A follow-up study of Medicare spending in the 1990s detected faster spending growth on behalf of low-income individuals (Lee, McClellan, and Skinner 1999).

The long-term significance of this trend was unclear, however, since it reflected increased home healthcare spending that was being reined in by the end of the decade, thus potentially "swing[ing] the redistributional effects of Medicare back in the other direction, towards the status quo of 1990" (105).

The conclusion that Medicare may be regressive on balance is based on an accounting measure of dollar flows, rather than on the value to recipients of what they get. If Medicare permits low-income retirees to have valuable health insurance that, due to some market failure, private insurers cannot offer them at an actuarially fair price, then an accounting measure understates their benefit from Medicare, and thus the program's true progressivity. On the other hand, the accounting measure overstates Medicare's value to low-income retirees, and thus perhaps its progressivity, to the extent that, due to other pressing needs, they would more frequently prefer cash to Medicare's in-kind benefits (McClellan and Skinner 1997, 47–48). Still, no matter how one evaluates these refinements to the pure accounting measure, it seems clear that Medicare is considerably less progressive than many people believe.

One-Earner Married Couples versus Other Households. Medicare also has little-recognized distributional effects between different kinds of households. In particular, it benefits one-earner married couples, such as traditional families in which the wife stays home, relative to two-earner couples and unmarried individuals. For the one-earned married couple, payroll and income taxes on one worker are followed by the receipt of retirement health insurance coverage for two—in effect, two for the price of one. The two-earner and single households must settle for two-for-two or one-for-one coverage. Indeed, the basic picture holds to a degree even if the stay-at-home spouse works just enough, in the course of her career, to qualify for her own Medicare benefits rather than simply getting them through marriage. She is still getting full coverage for relatively low payroll taxes.

This more favorable treatment of traditional families than of two-earner couples and singles augments similar biases elsewhere in the fiscal system. Both Social Security and the income tax provide one-earner couples with marriage bonuses that in effect transfer wealth to them from other types of households (Shaviro 2000a, 18–19, 57).

Health Differences. Medicare also has intragenerational distributional effects on people with differing health conditions and experiences. In particular:

1. Suppose Ann and Brenda are identical, except that Brenda faces greater health risks at retirement. By providing Ann and Brenda with retirement health insurance coverage for the same cost since they are otherwise identical, notwithstanding that Brenda figures to run up greater costs, Medicare redistributes in ex ante expected terms from Ann to Brenda—that is, from the low-risk to the high-risk.

2. Suppose Charles and David are identical, including in the health risks that they face at retirement, but that only David contracts an illness requiring costly treatment. Medicare redistributes from Charles to David—that is, from the healthy to the sick.

3. Suppose Edna and Fiona, otherwise identical, are comparably sick upon retirement, but that Fiona's condition is more treatable or costlier to treat. By paying more on behalf of Fiona, even though untreated she was not the worse-off of the two, Medicare redistributes from Edna to Fiona—that is, from the less (or more cheaply) treatable to the more (or more expensively) treatable.

4. Finally, suppose George and Harry are identical except that George dies in his sixties while Harry lives into his eighties. George ends up getting less from Medicare, despite having paid about the same taxes, unless the acceleration of his (typically high) near-death expenditures overweighs the fact that he is not in the system for as long. Indeed, if George dies before age sixty-five, he gets nothing from the program. Medicare thus most likely redistributes from George to Harry—that is, from the short-lived to the long-lived.

The last three of these distributional results all follow purely from the fact that Medicare is a retirement health insurance system. They would likewise be found under health insurance furnished by private businesses to voluntary subscribers (although, in the short-lived to long-lived case, this assumes up-front purchase of a whole-life retirement package, rather than periodic renewal). The first distributional result, however—redistribution from the low-risk to the high-risk—would not be found in private health insurance unless (1) people could insure before they knew their risk levels, (2) the insurance companies could not observe risk levels even if known to the subscribers, or (3) the companies were effectively barred by regulation from rejecting or charging higher premiums to the high-risk.

Regional Redistribution under Medicare. A final category of significant intragenerational Medicare redistribution is regional. Recent studies have found that, even controlling for various regional differences—such as the fact that the elderly often move to Florida or Arizona, or that some states are wealthier than others—households in some states do much better under Medicare (under an accounting measure of cash flows) than house-holds in other states. Thus, in Louisiana, the average household gains al-most $52,000 from Medicare on a lifetime basis, while in Hawaii the average household loses almost $20,000. Even further controlling for re-gional differences in disease burden, Medicare induces "federally-funded transfers of as much as $40,000 [per household] across states with similar income levels" (Feenberg and Skinner 2000, 714).

The main cause of these transfers appears to be regional differences in standard medical practice, and therefore in treatment intensity. In Miami, for example, a given medical condition typically prompts greater and cost-lier medical interventions than the same medical condition in Richmond or Minneapolis. The differences are great enough to suggest that "some regions must be doing something wrong; either Minneapolis and Rich-mond are providing too little medical care, or Miami is providing too much" (Skinner and Fisher 1997, 418).

Much of the underlying policy concern, therefore, should go to treat-ment appropriateness in different regions, rather than to what we think of a federal cash flow from Richmond to Miami. For example, if Richmond has it right, in the sense that patients there do just as well with its cheaper treatment, then the problem is one of waste in Miami, rather than of un-duly benefiting its Medicare enrollees. Likewise, if Miami has it right, then the problem is one of treatment inadequacy in Richmond. Tentative evi-dence that the problem is one of waste in high-cost areas emerges from surveys suggesting higher customer satisfaction in low-cost areas (Skinner and Fisher 1997, 418), along with the difficulty of detecting either im-proved health outcomes or distinctive consumer preferences in high-cost areas (Feenberg and Skinner 2000, 728–29).

Redistribution within One's Own Lifespan

So much for the main redistributive effects of Medicare both between and within generations. One final redistributive effect is intrapersonal, or from yourself when you are young and pay the taxes, to when you are old and get the benefits. You can try up to a point to reverse this redistribu-tion, such as by reducing other saving for your retirement. But you will likely find it impossible to dissipate the value of your Medicare coverage, such as by borrowing against it in order to consume more during your working years. No lender would make such a loan, given the impossibility of collecting on it.

As a semantic matter, one could question calling this "redistribution," since we may think of ourselves when young and when old as the same people. Certainly many who save for their retirement may think that they are helping themselves, rather than being altruistic toward some distinct future self. On the other hand, some commentators advocate a multiple-selves view of people as they age. Thus, Richard Posner (1995, 295) suggests: "Not through short-sightedness, but through sheer indifference, the young self may abandon his future old self. Compelled savings for retirement, like refusals to enforce suicide pacts and efforts to discourage harmful addictions, may reflect society's unwillingness to treat the current self as the 'owner,' for all purposes, of the body of which he is the temporary tenant."

It ends up making little bottom-line difference whether we take Posner's provocative tack, or instead think of people as myopic when they save what seems to be too little given their likely future needs. However, calling Medicare redistribution from yourself when young to when old serves a useful semantic purpose even under a one-self view of aging. It helps dramatize the fact that, in a world of scarcity, getting healthcare benefits is at the expense of getting something else you might have valued.

Medicare is often called an "entitlement," and healthcare when we are old a "right." This language is misleading, however, because it actually involves a mandatory personal budget choice. Suppose you lived alone like Robinson Crusoe. Would healthcare be a "right"? Perhaps the Universe would agree, and gratuitously give you more when you had greater health needs, but this seems unlikely. So, if you had a rule that all of your healthcare needs must be satisfied without regard to cost, what you actually would have decided is to misallocate your limited budget in cases where the healthcare you gave yourself was not worth its cost.

Now return to considering a mass society, like the United States. The same analysis holds to the extent that each of us is both paying for healthcare and receiving it. The language of entitlement begs the question: if the government required you to go out to dinner once a week, would the dinners that you ate but also paid for (whether you wanted them or not) be "entitlements"?

Admittedly, the mass society example differs from the Robinson Crusoe example in that it involves redistribution. We may on balance applaud the redistribution, and perhaps the language of "entitlement" is politically convenient in advancing it. Yet the sense in which the term may be misleading should not be entirely forgotten.

Summary

Probably the biggest incentive issue posed by Medicare pertains to seniors' cost consciousness at the margin in seeking healthcare, which actually becomes zero with certain Medigap coverage. While the decision to seek healthcare is often unavoidable as a consequence of one's condition, empirical evidence such as the RAND study suggests that it is by no means fixed. Thus, Medicare may frequently pay more for healthcare than its value to the recipient. Whether this is actually wasteful depends on what other reasons we might have for offering healthcare rather than cash.

A second incentive issue relates to healthcare providers, who may sacrifice patients' or taxpayers' best interests in pursuit of their own financial or other objectives. Agency cost problems are inherent in healthcare, just as in automobile repair, because diagnosticians are also paid for treatment. Ethical practice norms may help considerably, but also in some instances may actually encourage overtreatment.

A further set of incentive issues raised by Medicare goes to its likely adverse effect on the level of work and saving in our society. While this is par for the course in our fiscal system, one might be especially concerned about it if work and saving have positive externalities.

On the distributional side, Medicare's wealth transfer from younger to older generations has been paramount. It adds little if any progressivity within an age cohort, although many may misperceive it in this regard. It adds to the fiscal system's bias in favor of one-earner married couples, such as traditional families where the wife stays home. And it has the ex post distributional effects of private health insurance (such as aiding the sick at the expense of the healthy), plus it aids individuals who face high medical risk since the cost of its coverage is not risk-adjusted.

Since Medicare only finances consumption of a given type at a given point in the lifecycle, it is in some ways not an "entitlement" so much as a limitation on personal choice (taking its income effects as given). Thus, an important issue in evaluating Medicare is why we might want to limit people's choices, as the program clearly does.

4

A Five-Part Conceptual Decomposition of Medicare

WHILE the last two chapters covered Medicare's tax and benefit rules and its main incentive and distributional effects, a key bit of background is still missing. We need to get a better handle on what broader purposes the program really is serving or might be expected to serve. Why should we have a federal program that offers healthcare to seniors, and what should such a program be accomplishing? To answer this question, we need to break things down a bit. Rather than just discuss "Medicare," we should consider the constituent subprograms that make it up. And by this I mean not the policy wonk jargon of Parts A and B, but something more functional and fundamental.

A useful first step in this conceptual decomposition is to divide Medicare into its two distinct (albeit in practice integrated) parts as both a retirement system for all Americans and a single-payer national healthcare system for seniors. That is, it gives you something starting at age sixty-five, and what it gives you is heavily subsidized healthcare coverage, resembling that which many other economically developed countries offer to all of their citizens. As we will, see, however, each of these two main conceptual components of Medicare can then be additionally decomposed.

Medicare as a Retirement System

The Three Components of Medicare's Retirement Program

In analyzing Medicare purely as a retirement system, it is useful for most purposes to adopt the operating assumption that enrollees benefit by the full amount spent on their behalf. Thus, in this section I for the most part treat the payments that Medicare in fact makes to healthcare providers for covered services as if they instead went directly to the enrollees with no strings attached. These two alternatives would indeed have identical allocative and distributional effects if seniors who were given cash would use it to buy exactly the same services as those they actually get through Medicare. While this is unlikely to be the case, counterfactually assuming it here helps to isolate the pure retirement-system aspects of Medicare. The important consequences of the fact that Medicare actually offers in-kind benefits, via payment to healthcare providers, are best considered in relation to its second set of functions as a national healthcare system for seniors.

If an enrollee, with an eye to the consequences for her, looked at Medicare as mandating a set of cash flows between her and the government, two main questions would be of interest. The first is: "How do I fare overall?" That is, how do the payments you make compare in value to those that you get? The second is: "When do I pay and get paid?" And here, of course, the central point is that you help pay for Medicare when you work, but then it pays you when you retire.

The answer to the second question affects the first question because of the time value of money. Suppose, for example, that you paid Medicare a dollar at age twenty-five and got it back with zero interest at age sixty-five. If the after-tax interest rate were 6 percent, this would involve losing more than 90 percent of the value of your contribution. A $1 investment at age 25 would have grown to $10.30 over the next forty years at this interest rate, and a 9.72 cent investment at age twenty-five would have grown to a dollar. Thus, nominally breaking even is not good enough. Only if the cash you get from Medicare equals the taxes you paid plus the interest rate that you could have earned on these taxes have you really broken even in substance.

The importance of comparing your taxes to your benefits in light of the time value of money, elementary though it may seem, suggests decomposing Medicare's retirement program into two distinct parts. Suppose we use the following terms: T for your Medicare taxes, B for your Medicare benefits, and r for the interest rate that you could have earned by investing those taxes. Then, we would say that you have broken even through Medicare if $B = T + rT$.

Under a retirement healthcare program very different from the existing one, this equation might actually describe the set of cash flows that an individual participant would experience. Thus, suppose that Medicare were replaced by a system of mandatory "medical savings accounts" (MSAs), whereby each individual used her own contributions, perhaps invested at her own discretion, to pay for the health insurance that she would get at age sixty-five. Moreover, suppose the accounts were liquidated at that point to buy their holders lifetime health insurance packages with a value that depended on the account balance. Then the accounting equivalence of B to $T + rT$ would always hold.

In actual Medicare, however, the value of the insurance coverage depends neither on the Medicare taxes you paid nor on any set of investment outcomes with respect to particular funds. You therefore may gain or lose from Medicare overall, although it would be difficult to specify an equation describing its entire transfer policy. Rather than attempt this, we can simply add a placeholder to the equation. Let X connote the amount that must be added to the right side of the equation in order for it to balance. If positive it is a transfer to you; if negative (because $T + rT$ exceeded B) then it is a transfer from you to others. With this extra term, we now can use the following equation to describe any individual's Medicare experience:

$$B = T + rT + X.$$

This, of course, is a pure tautology. It holds in all cases simply because we define X as the amount needed to balance the equation. What makes it a useful tautology—a way of separating conceptually distinct elements in the system—is the fact that individuals, if they could borrow and lend at r, would only care about X.[1]

Bland and minimal though this basic Medicare equation may seem, it provides a handy lens for identifying several components of the program's retirement system. Among other things, the equation helps illustrate the fact that this retirement system is really three separate subprograms wrapped together. First, it is a system of forced saving, insofar as it requires workers to contribute T today in exchange for B in the future, or at least to defer receiving B. Second, it is a system of limiting portfolio choice, or the ability to decide how r will (at least implicitly) be determined. Third, it is a redistributive program, insofar as it shifts resources from people with a negative X to those with a positive X.

These three subprograms are distinct in the sense that having one of them need not imply having others. Thus, one or more of the subprograms could be revised or even scrapped while others remained the same. Each therefore merits separate examination.

Medicare and Forced Saving

So far as the forced saving element is concerned, actual Medicare works somewhat like an MSA. You pay the government, and even though your payments are not set aside in an individual account bearing your name, they are followed by a set of payments from the government to you when you retire. The fact that you may also be making or getting a transfer makes no fundamental difference to the character of the forced saving, but complicates describing it.

Even in an MSA system with no transfers, the measure of your forced saving at any time is not just T. Rather it is $T + rT$, since presumably you cannot withdraw before retirement either your contributions or the account's earnings. But more important still is the fact that, in either actual Medicare or an MSA system with transfers between accounts, a positive X must be saved as well. And when X is negative, the amount you are being forced to save is reduced. Since you will never get this money, we cannot say that you are being forced to wait for it.

Having to wait for the money—or rather, for the consumption opportunities that money can purchase—is exactly what "saving" means. It thus should be clear that Medicare has a forced saving element even for an individual who contributes nothing to the system (such as a 1966 retiree or a spouse who never works), and thus whose retirement healthcare is funded entirely by transfers from other taxpayers. Even that individual is saving relative to having gotten the money before age sixty-five (or in full upon reaching that age).

In two respects, this forced saving aspect of Medicare is easy to misunderstand. First, what it requires is a certain level of saving by a participant through the Medicare system (taking as given its transfer content). How Medicare affects her overall saving—presumably the point of greater interest—is analytically distinct. Second, the forced saving that Medicare requires is by a given individual. Thus, even if it does imply an increase to her saving, it need not increase saving by society as a whole.

On the first of these points, Medicare's true net effect on your consumption path over time depends on more than the timing of your cash flow interactions with it. Suppose, for example, that you could at all times freely borrow and lend at r, including by borrowing at any time against B's entire present value. Then Medicare would have no effect on your opportunity to time your lifetime consumption as you liked. For example, if you wanted to reach age sixty-five with zero retirement saving, all you would have to do is borrow against your Medicare (and Social Security) benefits, leaving you once you got there with debts that ate up your entire cash flow from the government's twin retirement systems. If we added as well the hypothesis that you would behave like the standard rational actor in neoclassical economics—optimizing given your preferences without regard to where you started from—then you certainly would do this if you liked, and Medicare's forced saving aspect would be completely irrelevant.

For two important reasons, this scenario does not accurately describe the actual Medicare system. First, given that Medicare actually pays third-party healthcare providers for certain covered services, rather than paying the enrollees themselves, borrowing against B would appear to be impossible. (At best, B may reduce the lender's concern about your dissipating other assets to pay for retirement healthcare.) Thus, Medicare is likely to succeed in creating a floor on the amount of retirement saving that you can have at age sixty-five, roughly equaling the value of B at that time. This means that Medicare should succeed in increasing overall retirement savings by individuals who otherwise would have saved less than B. (And this may well be a very large group, given evidence of Americans' frequently low propensity to save.)

Second, given that people do not always behave like neoclassical optimizers, Medicare may affect their overall retirement saving even if they save outside of Medicare. The principle of behavioral economics that people's decisions are highly sensitive to labeling and framing effects has by now gained wide acceptance (Shaviro 2000b, 22–25). So Medicare's set-aside of B might conceivably lead you to reduce your outside saving by less (or, for that matter, more) than B, relative to the case where it did not have a forced saving element.

In sum, the fact that Medicare forces you to save B through the system does not immediately tell us how it affects your overall retirement saving. B is, however, likely to serve at least as a floor on your retirement saving, and may affect your other saving. All this, however, concerns Medicare's effect on saving by a given individual—as distinct from its effect on national saving. Even as to a given individual, it takes as given Medicare's transfer content, which might affect the amount of saving. And it ignores the question of whether someone else—say, the custodian of B before it is paid out—is likely to consume more than if B had been paid out immediately. For these reasons, even if we agreed that every American's retirement saving either increases or stays the same by reason of having to wait for B, the system could still end up reducing national saving on balance.

This point can be illustrated through a simple hypothetical. Suppose we have a two-person society, composed of Adam and Brenda. Without any need to work, they each receive manna from the sky, which they can eat now or save for later. Adam, however, always eats immediately whatever manna he has on hand. If Brenda takes some of Adam's manna today in exchange for manna in the future, then Adam is being forced to save. Yet there need not be any overall saving, since Brenda can eat this manna plus all of her own. In that case, she would be offsetting Adam's saving through her own dissaving (in the sense that she has accumulated a future obligation to pay him). Society as a whole would be saving zero, just as it would be if both individuals ate all of their own manna. This illustrates what one might call the "custodian effect" on Brenda of deferring the payment to Adam of B.

The analogy between this hypothetical and the actual Medicare system is quite close. Suppose that levying Medicare taxes, and thus increasing the officially reported budget surplus (even net of Medicare expenditures) causes Congress to spend more than it would otherwise. If the spending is for current consumption, then the custodian effect likely reduces national saving, thus negating some or all of the increase in saving that results from beneficiaries' having to wait for *B*.

Now consider a hypothetical with income effects. Robinson Crusoe lives alone on a deserted island, collecting coconuts. Some of them he saves, so that he will have something left to eat when he is old and feeble. It then occurs to him that he is likely to be joined in the future by other shipwreck victims. So, as monarch of the island and possessor of a firearm, he pronounces that any subsequent castaways must support him when he retires. Suppose that he really can be confident his pronouncement will hold. A natural response might be to eat all the coconuts he gathers, thus consuming more and saving less than previously. Future shipwreck victims are unlikely, however, to offset this by accumulating in advance a few extra coconuts just so they will be ready. Accordingly, while the income effects of his pronouncement must be symmetric, the saving responses are not.

Once again, we have a close analogy to Medicare. Older generations that receive large transfers through the system respond to the expansion of their available lifetime resources by consuming more during their working years or early in retirement. Younger and future generations that pay for the transfers cannot, however, respond simultaneously by consuming less, since they are not yet on the scene.

For these reasons, the actual Medicare system has surely reduced national saving on balance since its inception. There is one offsetting factor, however. For individuals who receive employer-provided health insurance that they cannot trade in for a higher cash wage, Medicare may tend to induce earlier retirement (at age sixty-five rather than later). Once you qualify for Medicare, the value to you of your employer-provided health insurance, and thus of the entire compensation package, may decline. And if you anticipate that Medicare will induce you to retire a bit earlier than you would have otherwise, you may respond by saving more during your working years. After all, a longer retirement period implies a need for greater retirement savings (and fewer years of work in which to accumulate them).[2]

Medicare and Limited Portfolio Choice

To describe how Medicare affects portfolio choice, comparison to an MSA may once again help. Suppose you were required to make MSA contributions during your working years, which you then could invest however you liked, with the proceeds to be used, no later than when you turned sixty-five, to purchase health insurance coverage taking effect at that point. The account balance at age sixty-five would determine how much coverage you could afford. This would be a system with full portfolio choice, subject only to the ban on withdrawing the funds for earlier or nonmedical consumption.

The other polar design alternative would be to offer MSA holders no portfolio choice. Actual Medicare accomplishes this by offering what purports to be a universal defined-benefit (DB) plan. While in a sense the benefits are not fixed, since they are subject to technological risk (what services are actually available when you retire) and political risk (what Congress does to the program), there is still no individual choice within Medicare concerning how to address these risks. A defined-contribution (DC) plan could also in theory deny all portfolio choice. Suppose, for example, that all MSAs had to be invested in a specified fashion, or that the return on investments by the Part A Trust Fund would determine what Part A benefits were available to seniors in a given age cohort.

Investors may subjectively value portfolio choice for either of two reasons. Their beliefs about particular investments may differ from those suggested by market prices, or they may have distinctive risk preferences. In general, because most people are risk averse given the declining marginal utility of money, investments that are subject to greater variance must offer greater expected returns to attract investors. Accordingly, those of equal appeal in the marketplace can be plotted across what economists call the "risk-return frontier." This might take the visual form of a graph with risk on the horizontal axis and return on the vertical axis. The "frontier" is the line drawn by connecting the points that plotted the necessary (and continually increasing) return at each increasing risk level.[3]

While two same-size investments that are both on the risk-return frontier have, by definition, the same market value, not all investors regard them as equal. Some may favor riskier, higher-return overall portfolios than others. This, in turn, may reflect differences in either their preferences or their circumstances. For example, compensated risk may become more attractive to you as your wealth or earning ability increases, thus giving you a larger cushion to fall back on.

In saving for retirement health insurance (as for any other purpose), either of these considerations might cause individuals to differ in their investment preferences. For example, one might favor and another dislike having the value of the insurance package that they could purchase at age sixty-five depend on the performance of the stock market. Or one individual might want to lock in a given health insurance package years in advance—based, for example, on a belief that her health will be worse than expected or that the health sector will grow faster than expected—while a second prefers to wait.

In assessing the significance of Medicare's limits on portfolio choice, we must keep in mind the same cautionary note as with respect to its forced saving. All that the system can do is limit your investment of B. In theory, a sophisticated investor with sufficient assets or ability to borrow could adjust her outside portfolio in order to reverse any undesired effects of this implicit investment on her overall financial position. For example, if she did not want the value of her portfolio at retirement to depend on the growth of the healthcare sector, she could decide, in effect, to negate B's impact by going short or holding anti-B as well. In its purest form, this might involve selling a novel type of bond under which her payments to the holder would equal whatever Medicare paid on her behalf. Or she might more moderately bet against growth of the healthcare sector (which increases the value of B) by issuing a contingent debt instrument, offering payoffs that would rise with the growth rate of that sector.

These possibilities are not meant to be realistic. Indeed, more the reverse, in that their very implausibility helps to dramatize that Medicare actually affects people's overall retirement positions. We should keep in mind, however, that the point of real interest is not people's financial position through Medicare considered in isolation, but how it affects their overall positions. This, in turn, depends on such factors as their liquidity, financial sophistication, access to complete financial markets, and psychological commitment to pursuing a consistent set of overall investment objectives.

Medicare as a Redistributive Program

Medicare's distributional policy provides one last occasion for comparing it to a retirement healthcare plan that used mandatory MSAs. An MSA system can include whatever transfers one likes, through either of two mechanisms. The first is to mandate transfers from some accounts to others. The second is to regulate the price of the insurance coverage that MSAs are used to acquire—for example, by barring risk-adjusted pricing or requiring high-earners to pay more for the same coverage.

The main difference between redistribution via MSAs and existing Medicare is that the MSA route might involve greater specification of what the distributional policy actually is. For example, if money is added to or extracted from a given individual's MSA, then the distributional effect on her is pretty clearcut. Under Medicare, by contrast, many of the distributional outcomes are obscure and widely misunderstood. People may be inclined, for example, to assume that all current retirees have fully paid for their benefits even if this is far from being the case. Or they may overlook the transfer to one-earner married couples, since it is not explicit.

The significance of having no clear tax-benefit relationship in Medicare depends on how this ends up affecting political outcomes. You might like the indirection, for example, in the case of transfers that you believed were good policy but feared would not be openly embraced by voters and Congress. And you would certainly dislike it in the case of transfers you opposed and thought could not stand sunlight. However, even if on balance the lack of a clear link is politically efficacious, it runs the risk of inducing redistribution that is accidental, and therefore potentially haphazard.

Medicare as a National Healthcare Plan for Enrollees

Turning to Medicare's second core program as a national healthcare system for enrollees, the fact that it provides in-kind benefits rather than cash moves to center stage, while the fact that it is only for seniors exits at stage right. Many of the reasons why one might want to offer such a program to seniors—say, because healthcare is too important to be denied to people who cannot afford it—generalize to the entire population. Medicare was indeed first proposed as a pragmatically chosen first step toward the incremental creation of national healthcare (Marmor 2000, 10), drawing on solicitude for the elderly and the popularity of Social Security to defuse political opposition to "socialized medicine."

Medicare's national healthcare program, like its retirement program, can usefully be decomposed. At any given moment when you are covered by national healthcare, looking forward you have insurance coverage. Unpredictable medical treatment needs will not cost you money to the extent of your coverage. Looking back over a given period, however, what you have gotten, upon the resolution of this uncertainty, is an actual set of healthcare services.

These are not distinct subprograms in the same sense as the three components of Medicare's retirement system. Insurance up front implies paying certain expenses down the road, and promising to pay them if incurred implies insurance. We therefore could not have one of the two national healthcare subprograms without the other. Nonetheless, distinguishing between the two programs is expositionally useful. They bring to the fore distinct motivations: responding to uncertainty in the case of the insurance, and to the special status of healthcare needs in the case of actual payment. In addition, Medicare's insurance features encourage a different inquiry than its healthcare features—one that focuses on such issues as what copayments it requires as distinct from what services fit the rationale for giving healthcare favored status.

Medicare as a System of Paying for Healthcare

A decision to have the government pay for healthcare requires determining exactly what sorts of procedures we want to cover. The category is not self-defining. A popular dictionary sends us merrily in a circle by defining health as "physical or mental well-being [or] freedom from disease," and disease (via illness) as "the condition of being in poor health." Medicine, meanwhile, involves "treating and preventing disease," along with "relieving pain" (Neufeldt and Sparks 1995).

Circularities notwithstanding, all this conveys the basic idea of a normal or baseline state of physical and mental welfare, which then is impaired by the threatened or actual onset of some painful or disabling pathology. That pathology is then addressed with the aim of restoring normality.

We tend to regard healthcare as very important because, if the pathology threatens us with pain, suffering, disability, or death, we might be willing to pay a huge or even infinite amount to alleviate it. This may suggest being considerably more distressed when someone else cannot afford medical treatment than when she must go without, say, restaurant meals or a car. Thus, suppose we hear of a cancer sufferer who could be greatly helped by a costly treatment, but lacks the money to pay for it. We might readily believe each of two things. First, the money needed for the treatment seems likely to have greater subjective value to her than to someone who merely wanted, for example, to engage in luxurious living. Second, she seems likely to be worse off than people who are otherwise similarly situated but do not have cancer. Thus, having the government pay for her healthcare might be viewed both as directing resources to where the need for them is greater and as helping the worse-off relative to the better-off.

Not everyone accepts this welfare economics-inflected view of healthcare. "Medicalists" (in Sherry Glied's terminology) believe that healthcare should be completely egalitarian, with the rich getting no more or better care than the poor, in sharp distinction to how most other goods and services are allocated in our society (Glied 1997, 29). This follows from a "deep-seated belief . . . that medical care is not a commodity, that its characteristics are scientifically determined, and that decisions concerning it must be entrusted to professionals" (Havighurst 1990, 419). In this view, government provision of healthcare keeps the market's grasping hands from reaching where they do not belong, and ensures that price and cost considerations will not influence consumer demand.

The genuine differences between these two views may unduly obscure what they have in common. Presumably, medicalists, even though they purport to ignore actual consumer demand, rely on the view that people who face pain, suffering, disability, or death can be greatly helped by an effective treatment and/or are likely to be worse off than the healthy. Under either approach, therefore, government coverage for a given treatment or service ought to bear some relationship to its expected effect on patients' well-being.

Various goods or services that healthcare providers offer do not fit comfortably within either a welfare-based or a medicalist view of what the government ought to cover. Representative examples include the following:

• The cost of room and board for a hospital stay, at least if they are nicer than was medically necessary (such as a private room, chosen to satisfy a taste for privacy.) The broader problem here is one of intermingling between medical and other personal living expenses, where the latter are furnished in relation to providing the former.

• Treatment for relatively minor pathologies, defects, or physical attributes, to serve social or aesthetic preferences or the pursuit of leisure. Although the scope of this category is debatable, examples might include plastic surgery for someone who is not disfigured, elective arthroscopic surgery so one can play recreational sports, and taking Viagra to improve sexual performance. In these cases, the subjective benefit may have more in common with that from ordinary consumer expenditures than with curing cancer.

• Intensive medical treatment near the end of one's life, if it offers little or no benefit. An example might be "the use of radical prostatectomy for invasive prostate cancer" despite its unclear impact on the quality and length of life (Garber, MaCurdy, and McClellan 1998, 247). End-of-life treatment is a recent hot topic in Medicare research, reflecting evidence that more than 20 percent of program expenditures are for people who die within the year (Lubitz and Riley 1993), although this does not mean that predictably futile expenditure is common or can be identified.

Any healthcare system, whether it be Medicare or private health insurance, must deal with issues such as these. They help to illustrate several points that should be kept in mind when evaluating government-provided healthcare. First, in some instances we may need to think further about the relative weight we attach to aiding the people we can help the most, as opposed to aiding those who are worst-off (such as the very sick who are not very treatable). Second, medical expenditure in common usage may be considerably broader than the category of items that (like curing cancer) most strongly motivate government provision. Third and relatedly, we should recognize how frequently the goods and services that emanate from the healthcare industry present us with shades of gray, in addition to being potentially intermingled with other sorts of consumption goods. Healthcare permits varying degrees of improvement, from varying starting and ending points, to varying physical and mental functions or capacities that people value and use in diverse ways.

Health Insurance

A final Medicare subprogram is its providing health insurance to enrollees. To the extent of their coverage, they are not affected out-of-pocket by variation in the amount of healthcare that they end up needing. To help us in ultimately evaluating this subprogram, I briefly consider the general nature of insurance.

Ambrose Bierce gave the cynic's definition, calling insurance an "ingenious modern game of chance in which the player is permitted to enjoy the comfortable conviction that he is beating the man who keeps the table" (Bierce 1993 ed., 63). This would indeed be the explanation if the highly variable outcomes of the "bets" it involves—as when you either have a highway smashup and win thousands of dollars from the automobile insurance company, or else drive safely so that your policy proves a dud—stood alone, rather than offsetting other undesired bets that your circumstances caused you to make.

Given the offset to these other bets, however, people often willingly accept a negative return from insurance, in the form of a premium that exceeds the expected payoff. A negative-return insurance bet can increase your expected utility or satisfaction despite reducing your expected income. Often this reflects declining marginal utility, or the tendency of each additional dollar to be worth less to you than the dollar before, since you presumably satisfy your most urgent needs first. Thus, in the car insurance case, although a million dollars would always have been welcome, you are especially glad to get it if you otherwise would face financial ruin.

The value of a negative-return insurance bet may also reflect that a bad outcome (while not directly costing you anything) would give you a new need that increased money's value to you. An example is an automobile accident that smashed your legs, if a million-dollar operation could restore full functioning. At the margin, money can now improve your circumstances more than it could have before the injury. And this new need (which medicine happens to be able to address), rather than merely the fact that the accident and its aftermath were horrendously unpleasant, provide the reason for your wanting insurance coverage. This is why, for example, we do not observe single individuals without dependents buying much life insurance. Even if death is the worst thing that can happen to them, extra money in that state of affairs would not help.

The point that the value of money depends on what you can buy with it at a given time can hold equally even if nothing bad has recently happened to you. Consider the case of a tennis player with a congenitally bad shoulder, facing uncertainty about whether an arthroscopic procedure will be developed that can help him, at the moment when he must select a health insurance package for the next ten years. Under the good outcome in which a suitable procedure is developed, he will want more generous healthcare coverage than under the bad outcome where he cannot be helped. Thus, he may insure "against" the good outcome by selecting more costly and generous coverage than he would have preferred in the absence of hope. He therefore in effect transfers money from himself in the bad future state of the world (where he ends up overpaying for the services he gets) to himself in the good future state of the world (where he ends up using the coverage to pay for the surgery).

This phenomenon of insuring against "good" outcomes, in the sense of those where you can be helped, is common in health insurance—perhaps more so than for most insurance. One cannot readily see, for example, the car insurance analogue. In the case of health insurance, however, any reasonable person who (in the absence of Medicare, or due to its coverage gaps) is considering how costly a package she will want at retirement ought to take into account the trend in medical technology of ever-expanding treatment options. In the MSA scenario, for example, it would make sense to invest more in your account than otherwise given the possibility that, when you retire, there may be costly yet valuable new procedures such as cancer cures. This point is quite important to the issue of long-term Medicare design.

Summary

Medicare is easier to analyze if we break it into its component subprograms, rather than trying to grapple with it as a single multipurpose abstraction. As an initial step, we can divide it into a retirement program and a national healthcare program. Then the retirement program can be broken into three parts: forced saving, limited portfolio choice, and redistribution of various kinds. The national healthcare program can be divided into two parts: paying for certain healthcare, and providing enrollees with health insurance.

The forced saving component of Medicare arises from the fact that people generally cannot consume the present value of their benefits from the system before age sixty-five. Even though they can respond to this component by reducing their saving outside the system, Medicare surely succeeds in requiring a minimum level of retirement saving by enrollees (taking as given the program's transfer content), equal to the value of its coverage at retirement. At the same time, due primarily to Medicare's income effects and in particular its transferring wealth to older from younger generations, it has almost certainly reduced national saving since its enactment.

Medicare limits portfolio choice by requiring that you invest in an implicit financial instrument, the value of which depends on such variables as your medical condition, the growth of the healthcare sector, and the program's political and financing risk over the relevant period. As in the case of forced saving, you may respond outside the system by adjusting your other investments. Nonetheless, the system probably has a substantial effect on millions of Americans' overall financial positions, if only by reason of how many people enter retirement without substantial independent savings and would not otherwise insure.

Medicare's redistributive program is relatively opaque due to the lack of an explicit link between the Medicare taxes you pay and the value at age sixty-five of the coverage that you get. Among other consequences, this structure may cause people to underestimate the transfer to older generations (members of whom may believe they paid for their benefits), overestimate Medicare's progressivity, and simply miss the transfer to one-earner married couples from other households.

Medicare's program of paying for certain healthcare expenses of enrollees may reflect our view that people who incur such expenses tend both to be worse-off than others and to benefit more from an extra dollar in their pocket (since they can use it to buy restored health). This view is compelling if we consider the case of an individual who is suffering from a potentially deadly cancer that can be treated effectively but at great cost. We should not, however, overgeneralize about the extent to which healthcare expenditures, within common usage, have this character. Nicer hospital rooms and elective surgery, for example, may have more in common with ordinary consumer expenditure.

Medicare's health insurance diversifies the risk of getting sick, just as car insurance diversifies the risk of having a costly accident. While this is insurance against a bad outcome, Medicare also provides insurance against a good outcome—the risk that your health problems will become more treatable, albeit at an increased cost, leading you to want more healthcare coverage.

5

Medicare's Social Insurance and Risk Prevention Purposes

Reasons for Government Intervention

EVEN identifying Medicare's five subprograms does not immediately elucidate why we might want such a system. The last missing piece of the analysis concerns the reasons for government intervention. Each subprogram other than redistribution involves something that people can seemingly do on their own if they want. Given their lifetime incomes and subject to the completeness of various markets, they can decide for themselves how much to save for retirement, how to invest this saving, how much retirement health insurance to carry, and what benefits the insurance should cover. So why would the government step in, to compel either choices that people can make for themselves or redistribution that the losers would not voluntarily agree to?

In general, there are two principal justifications for government intervention. The first relies on missing or incomplete markets, which prevent people from getting the things we surmise they want. Here the aim is to expand choice by supplementing what private markets offer. This is the rationale for supplying public goods, such as national defense, that private firms could not offer due to the "holdout" problem that arises when benefits cannot be limited to subscribers.

The second justification, however, involves restricting choice by compelling people to do A rather than B, on the ground that otherwise they might choose wrongly. Here the concern is either that they are ill equipped to make wise choices for themselves or that they face the wrong incentives from an aggregate social standpoint. For an example of this type of intervention, consider drunk driving bans and speed limits. Presumably, the rationale for penalizing people who violate these rules, even for what they decide are good and sufficient reasons, is that we believe they may be unduly endangering themselves and others.

Most discussion of Medicare seems to place it squarely in the first category of market supplementation. Thus, it is invariably classified as a "social insurance" program, or one that seeks to extend the risk-sharing

function of private insurance to areas where market failure would otherwise prevent people from getting the personal security they want (Graetz
and Mashaw 1999, 16–17). As we will see, however, this is only part of
the Medicare picture, and possibly a smaller part than choice restriction of
the sort that underlies speed limits and drunk driving rules. To show this,
I start by considering the circumstances that may support market supplementation via social insurance.

The Case for and Character of Social Insurance

Market Failure in the Offering of Private Insurance

People face an enormous variety of risks in their lives that might make
insurance attractive. Consider the possibility that your house will lose
value or your job disappear due to broader economic factors. Private insurance markets nonetheless are quite incomplete; they cover only a hand-
ful of discrete, fairly dramatic risks such as dying, getting sick or injured,
being sued, and losing property in a fire.

Among the obstacles to offering private insurance more broadly are
moral hazard and *adverse selection*. Moral hazard arises when the insurer
cannot perfectly monitor actions by insured individuals that affect the oc-
currence or magnitude of a covered loss. An example is driving too fast or
under the effects of alcohol because you know that the company will pay
your accident costs if you crash. Insurers have a number of tools for addressing moral hazard. For example, they may impose deductibles that
deny coverage for a fixed dollar amount, along with coinsurance that requires the insured to bear a specified percentage of losses. Even so, moral
hazard can severely limit or even prevent the offering of insurance. Thus,
while companies can readily offer fire insurance for homes (despite the effect on incentives to prevent a fire), they may be unable to offer attrac-
tively priced insurance against the quite substantial economic risk of
having to sell your home for a loss. The problem here is that your actions
in home upkeep and sales strategy or effort are hard to monitor. The end
result may be that you are forced to bear an undesired risk that is in principle diversifiable, due to the difficulty of credibly guaranteeing your
good-faith effort to seek the best available price.

Adverse selection arises when the prospective purchasers of insurance
have better information than the insurer about their own risks. Thus, suppose that there are low-risk and high-risk individuals who know their own
identities but whom the insurance company cannot tell apart. Any effort
to offer insurance to low-risk individuals at a reasonable rate (given their
actual expected losses) will induce relative oversubscription by the high-

risk individuals, who know that at these odds they are indeed beating the man who keeps the table. The result may be that no one can be insured for a premium that is set below the high-risk individuals' expected loss.

Where these or other obstacles to the offering of private insurance on attractive terms are great enough, private insurance will not be found. One therefore can speak of incomplete private insurance markets that fail to satisfy people's demand for protection from risk. Without more, however, this is merely cause for regret, like the fact that ice cream is fattening or that dinner dishes do not wash themselves. Both as individual consumers and as a society, we must do without things that are unfeasible to provide or cost more than we are willing to pay for them.

What potentially creates a case for government intervention is some reason to think it can do better than private firms in addressing the obstacles to providing insurance on attractive terms. Yet one must also consider any special disadvantages of using the government to provide insurance. These might, for example, relate to administrative efficiency or political incentive structures.

While the government, if no more able than a private firm to monitor behavior, is no better situated to address moral hazard, it often is better positioned to address adverse selection. So long as it controls a large enough territory for exit to be costly, it can effectively require all or selected residents to enroll. This could, in principle, make all of the forced participants better off ex ante, or as judged prior to their having any information about their risk positions.

Income Risk and Social Insurance

The preeminent example of a risk that private insurance markets largely leave uncovered, despite the value of hedging it, is income risk, or the risk that, whether for a given period or over your entire life, your income will be low rather than high. The generally declining marginal utility of money suggests that you should be interested in insuring against having a low income by in effect betting against yourself as a worker—just as, by purchasing car insurance, you bet against yourself as a driver.

To be sure, if income were simply a function of how hard you decided to work, it would not be risky and thus you would not need to insure it. In practice, however, people are subject to income risk of at least two kinds. One is that unknown circumstances beyond their control may determine their success or failure after they have acted, such as by starting a particular business or acquiring a particular workplace specialization. Businesses unpredictably succeed or fail all the time, and professions from oil production to legal work on corporate mergers and acquisitions are subject to surprise gains or losses from market demand shocks and competition from other suppliers. An income-based tax-transfer system mitigates these risks (Varian 1980).

The second form of income risk involves what one might call the "ability lottery." People are born or somehow stumble (be it from nature or nurture) into varying abilities to convert effort into earnings. This could reflect their intelligence, looks, self-discipline, unscrupulousness, family connections, or whatever else makes some people economically more successful than others. So long as any uncertainty remains about your degree of good fortune in this regard, you are subject to a risk. Even once you know your "ability" level, however, it is natural to think: "I was lucky or unlucky in how this lottery came out." And by extension: "If I am risk-averse, I would have liked to insure against this risk had this been possible while I remained uncertain." Among public finance economists, at least since the Nobel Prize–winning work of James Mirrlees (1971), the income tax has been conceptualized as an insurance mechanism to mitigate undesired risk from people's involuntary participation in the ability lottery. That is, it seeks to transfer income from those more able to those less able, although since ability cannot be directly observed it relies instead on earnings (leading to moral hazard since earnings reflect work effort as well as ability).

This extension of insurance thinking may seem to push the envelope a bit. After all, the real world income tax is implemented under the direction of voters who pretty well know how the ability lottery has come out for them. What is more, people who were sufficiently well formed as individuals to make choices or even have preferences about insurance may inevitably have at least some inkling about the ability level that this notional lottery has dealt them. Yet, while these objections are pertinent to the question of how we should actually try, in an imperfect political world, to mitigate income risk through the tax-transfer system, at a basic conceptual level they can be disregarded. The idea of a "veil of ignorance," behind which you should make distributional judgments as if you did not know your own particular circumstances, underlies the case for an insurance view. This idea is usually attributed to the philosopher John Rawls (1971), but was earlier stated by the economist John Harsanyi (1953, 435), who justified it in terms of a morally required indifference between oneself and other people. To make a genuine value judgment about alternative income distributions, rather than simply expressing crass self-interest, you must disregard how you in particular (compared to other people) would be affected by the outcome. This in turn requires "asking what sort of society [you] would prefer if [you] had an equal chance of being 'put in the place of' any particular member of the society," which is no less a risk problem than deciding on car insurance.[1]

In sum, therefore, income risk is well worth insuring against as a way of increasing your expected utility across different possible states of the world. Private insurers, however, cannot address it more than minimally[2] due to adverse selection problems that a government may be well positioned to address.

The downside of using the government to address income risk must also be kept in mind, however. Insurance that is justified on the basis of hypothetical agreement from behind the veil may differ greatly from what the political system actually provides. Political outcomes inevitably reflect the interests of the actors given how things have turned out for them. The language of insurance can thus be misused in support of redistributive schemes that are entirely capricious, such as transferring wealth to farmers or homeowners, or for that matter to Saddam Hussein. People's differing views about the gravity of these dangers relative to the benefits of well-executed social insurance naturally produce disagreement about the likely social gain or loss from government activity in mitigating income risk.

Another Reason for Social Insurance?

Again, Harsanyi justifies social insurance on the ground that morally compelled indifference between individuals requires that you maximize your expected utility under the assumption that you have an equal chance of being put in the place of any particular member of the society. This standard leads to a utilitarian social welfare norm that has never commanded widespread acceptance.

One set of objections to utilitarianism, holding that factors apart from people's welfare are morally relevant, I will not consider, although it might affect one's view of Medicare. There also, however, are possible objections to utilitarianism within the "welfarist" tradition that looks exclusively at individuals' subjective well-being. In particular, utilitarianism often is criticized for not valuing equality of welfare as an end in itself. Since it values everyone's welfare equally, it would suggest, for example, taking a dollar from a homeless person and giving it to Bill Gates if one believed (perhaps implausibly) that this would increase Bill's happiness more than it would reduce that of the homeless person.

Some egalitarian welfarists seek to avoid this hypothetical implication of utilitarianism by arguing that the welfare of worse-off individuals should count for more than that of better-off individuals. Thus, in the above example, if we valued the homeless person's welfare twice as much as that of Bill Gates, we would not approve the regressive transfer unless we believed that Bill would enjoy possessing the dollar more than twice as much. In addition, and more pertinently, we would likely favor more redistribution from well-off to poorly-off individuals than under a straight utilitarian norm. The redistributive implications are especially strong if we adopt the strongest possible version of egalitarian welfarism—a "leximin" view, adapted from John Rawls (although he was not a welfarist), that treats the welfare of the worst-off individual as infinitely more important than that of anyone else.

This perhaps abstruse-sounding dispute within welfarism has important implications for Medicare policy, where it might affect the direction, rather than just the magnitude, of desirable transfers. For now, however, I note only that it might be thought of as providing an additional motivation for government intervention via the provision of social insurance. Under a view holding that worse-off people's welfare should have extra weight, we would buy too little income insurance, even if it were available before we had any information concerning our ability levels. The problem is that, by seeking to maximize our expected utility by directing extra dollars to states of the world where we expected to value them the most, we would be disregarding the assumed egalitarian grounds for assigning moral value to considerations other than our expected welfare. So the government would need to step in and correct this incentive problem (from the egalitarian standpoint) by providing more insurance than people would want for themselves individually.

Government-Mandated Risk Prevention

Why Override People's Choices?

One thing that private contractual arrangements, such as insurance, cannot do is force people to act against their preferences. People may contractually bind themselves to do something that might be against their preferences later on, but the initial agreement must be voluntary. The government, however, can use its superior force to impose restrictions on people, whether they like it or not. This power to make people eat their spinach—or, for that matter, their arsenic—gives the government an important and unique tool in societal risk management.

Where people face the risk of bad things happening to them, private insurers are limited to arranging bets between counterparties, typically made feasible by risk-spreading since there are not enough risk lovers to bet with all those who are risk averse. The government, however, can also engage in risk prevention, by forbidding behavior that would increase the likelihood of bad things happening in the first place. Yet, even for examples as uncontroversial as drunk driving bans and speed limits, it is worth asking why we would stop people from doing what they prefer. After all, even the drunk driver and the speeder may have decided quite deliberately that the risks they are taking the worth the benefits. They are anxious to get somewhere fast, for example, and may believe that, having escaped any harm from this behavior the last fifty times, they can count on doing so again.

If we care about people's well-being and believe that they usually act in their own best interests, there are only two grounds for overriding such decisions. The first is that, in these circumstances unlike many others, we do not believe that a given choice can rationally be defended as reflecting the true self-interest of the actor. Or at least we may believe that error is sufficiently likely and costly for a general prohibition to be justified. This is an argument of *paternalism*. Second, we may believe that the actor is sufficiently hurting the interests of others to justify imposing a ban. This is an argument about *externalities*, or consequences that the actor may be inclined to disregard because she does not bear them. Each ground merits further discussion.

Paternalism

Paternalism is often a dirty word, reflecting our concern that it may be too readily deployed without proper justification. The world is full of people who mistakenly think they know better than others do, and that whatever is good for them must surely be good for everyone. Some of these people go into politics.

Even among people (or at least adults) whom we know intimately, we should perhaps be cautious about assuming that we know best what is good for them. Sometimes, however, we may know enough about their personal characteristics and circumstances to venture to make such a judgment. Perhaps we are wiser or more experienced, or can step back and assess things more dispassionately. Even so, to so opine about the millions of strangers who would be subject to a given government mandate may seem considerably more dubious. How can we possibly know enough about them to second-guess their decisions from the standpoint of their own self-interest? The answer is twofold. We may have a theory of human behavior and psychology that makes particular types of errors seem likely.

And we may have a theory concerning what decisions are best, so that those who make a different choice seem likely to be in error.

Drunk driving rules and speed limits provide a ready illustration. We know (in part from introspection) that people may lack foresight and self-control, overrate their own abilities, and underestimate low probability events that they have not recently experienced.[3] In addition, we may surmise that the pleasures of being able to drinknd then drive home without special arrangements, or else of getting somewhere fast, are trivial compared to the harm of a collision. So we may be quite prepared to second-guess drunk and speeding drivers' judgment, based on our view of the odds along with the assumption that they must (or should) share our aversion to death and serious injury.

Paternalism, in short, has appeal as a judgment about particular situations, without requiring a broader claim that Big Brother knows best. Indeed, if we know that our own judgments are wobbly sometimes, the paternalism may be partly self-directed, rather than reflecting a sense of superiority to others. Just like an impulsive shopper who forces herself to save through a Christmas club, we may conclude that many or all of us tend to better make certain decisions in advance than in the heat of the moment. Paternalism may thus be a precommitment strategy rather than expressing deference to the superior wisdom of legislators or bureaucrats.

Externalities

The classic example of an externality that causes people's rationally self-interested decisions to have adverse social effects is pollution. In illustration, a factory owner who pollutes a nearby stream while making turbo-powered widgets may capture all of the profits from this activity while not bearing the pollution costs. Thus, Adam Smith's invisible hand, in guiding her production decisions, has a thumb on the scales (or missing from the scales). She is being induced to count the benefit to consumers that they communicate by buying the widgets, but not the detriment to those who suffer from the pollution.

While pollution is the classic textbook externality, the concept's reach is far broader. An externality exists whenever one person affects others' welfare in a manner that market prices fail to transmit (Rosen 1999, 86). Thus, people who play their radios loudly at a crowded beach are creating externalities (and positive ones if their neighbors like what they hear), despite the absence of anything so tangible as a factory emission. For that matter, if while at the beach you read Danielle Steele rather than Dostoevsky and this distresses a neighbor with more fastidious tastes, the case is conceptually the same as that of pollution if we rule out market responses such as her offering to pay you to switch.

Examples where one person's consumption choices affect other people's welfare simply because they care about what she consumes can often be dismissed as overly fanciful. Most people generally are not, one hopes, such busybodies as to care intensely about other people's consumption choices. However, preferences about other people's consumption actually are important to government transfer policy in certain settings.

We sometimes act on altruistic preferences for helping others, including strangers in distress. Yet our altruistic preferences need not amount to valuing the welfare of those we want to help in exactly the same way that they value it themselves. Instead, we may value helping them in one way but not another, based purely on our own differential identification or sympathy with them. Suppose that a homeless person requests money for food, though you suspect that she would use it instead to buy alcohol. While you might have paternalistic reasons for helping with food but not drink, you also might not value giving her the latter, even if she could persuade you that it would increase her subjective welfare more. So you genuinely value her welfare, but more selectively than she does.

Such targeted altruistic preferences have strongly influenced various government transfer programs. Consider Medicaid and Food Stamps, which provide beneficiaries with healthcare and food even if they would prefer to spend the money on something else. Interest group politics may help to explain these programs—the farm lobby, for example, provides crucial support for Food Stamps (Loomis 2000, 108)—but the programs also derive political appeal from their providing aid of a kind that voters like. From this perspective, the classic Milton Friedman (1962, 192) argument that all aid to the poor should be "in the form most useful to the individual, namely, cash" misses an important efficiency issue, unless we reinterpret it as an appeal to voters to alter their consumer preferences. Paying rent with money that other people (such as those who furnished it to you) would rather have seen you use for food involves an externality, within the preference-based usage of welfare economics, no less than polluting a stream.

IN SUM, paternalism and externalities provide important rationales for government policy that seeks to override people's choices in the interest of risk prevention, as distinct from risk-sharing. These rationales overlap with that for market-supplementing social insurance, since adverse selection could itself be called an externalities problem. The rationales begin to look quite different, however, when the issue is not just how much money a participant gets, but how she must spend it.

Assessing Medicare's Retirement Program as a Social Insurance and Risk Prevention System

To what extent does Medicare provide desirable social insurance and risk prevention? Here I evaluate the three subprograms that make up its retirement plan, under the simplifying (albeit false) assumption that Medicare benefits are equivalent to cash. I leave for the next section, discussing Medicare's national healthcare plan, the issues that are raised by its providing in-kind rather than cash benefits.

Forced Saving

Forced saving plainly is risk prevention, rather than mandatory risk-sharing. Thus, a key question raised by Medicare's forced saving component is why paternalism or externalities would justify frustrating the preferences of someone who would spend the money before retirement if given the chance.

The paternalist case for it can be stated in terms of the lifecycle model in economics (Modigliani and Brumberg 1954; Friedman 1957), which predicts that people will take a rationally farsighted view of how to allocate their consumption opportunities across their lifespans, rather than following the "eat when you kill" philosophy of the primordial savannah. The general implication is that you should smooth your consumption path relative to your earning path, since earnings fluctuate but you always need food, clothing, and shelter. Your medical needs, moreover, are likely to be greatest late in life, when you can no longer earn enough to pay for them. Given the prospect of retirement and increasing physical fragility, the lifecycle model strongly implies saving a significant fraction of income during your working years unless you expect to die young.

While the lifecycle model is sometimes treated as an empirical prediction derived from the rationality hypothesis, it is more persuasive as a normative account of what consumption and saving behavior would be rational. Studies suggest that people often violate lifecycle planning principles. For example, half of those in the middle income deciles approach retirement with little accumulation, and retirement often prompts sharp belt-tightening, almost as if it had come as a surprise (Shiller 1998, 42). Perhaps the savannah was a poor training ground for a world with today's life expectancies and saving vehicles.

The case for lifecycle saving creates an inference, even if one usually dislikes paternalism, that here people would benefit from being forced to do something that they fail to do on their own. Only those who would otherwise save less than the expected value of their Medicare benefits are adversely affected. And even if some of these people really are doing the best thing for themselves, it is plausible that most are helped.

An externalities argument makes sense here as well. If we are pained when the elderly cannot afford important healthcare, we may want to ensure that they spare us this sight by saving more earlier in their lives. In addition, if those who would "inflict" this sight on us can predict that we would pay to alleviate the problem when it arises, the altruistic externality turns back into conventional moral hazard. Now their forced saving saves us the extra money that we would pay if, having consumed in advance the value of their expected Medicare benefits, they could get us to pay for their retirement healthcare.

Thus, a forced saving program can sensibly require that people be in a position to meet their post-retirement healthcare needs. We should keep in mind, however, that Medicare accomplishes the forced saving in a manner that probably reduces national saving. When technological change increases the amount that we are likely to want to spend on our retirement healthcare, Medicare does not respond by making us save more of our own lifetime earnings. Rather, future generations foot the bill unless Congress promptly responds to the technological change by increasing Medicare or other taxes relative to spending. This leaves future generations with less to spend on their own healthcare needs (among other uses)—an effect that may be perverse if the trends make added healthcare expenditure more valuable still to them.

Limited Portfolio Choice

Limiting portfolio choice, like inducing forced saving, is social insurance via risk prevention, rationalized by paternalism with a dollop of moral hazard. Paternalism is supported by an account of rational investor choice that is powerful enough to suggest that violators are either misguided or counting on rescue by the public fisc.

This notion of rational investor choice has two components pertaining to overall portfolios and specific investments. Under the former, overall risk should be limited through diversification, and perhaps by holding some investments that offer relatively fixed and safe returns. Under the latter, one should not pick bad investments, or those lying inside the risk-return frontier, and thus offering too little return for the risk and too much risk for the expected return.

Persuasive though these guiding principles are, investors frequently violate them. Classic recent examples include people who failed to anticipate the collapse of the Internet bubble of the late 1990s, and Enron employees who took their bosses' advice to bet on the company's future without diversifying.

By offering what is nominally a defined-benefit (DB) plan, albeit subject to political and technological risk, Medicare prevents people from investing *B* (the accrued value of their expected benefits) in such an ill-advised way as to chance reaching age sixty-five without sufficient assets to purchase adequate health insurance. Time will tell, however, whether this investment actually proves as safe as expected. One also could argue that an element of risk, permitting a higher expected return, would benefit some participants.

Redistribution through Medicare

Generational Redistribution. Medicare's redistributive subprogram places us at last firmly in the realm of risk-spreading and market supplementation (albeit made mandatory due to adverse selection). However, before evaluating the program's largest redistribution, from younger to older generations, one must ask whether it actually affects bottom-line outcomes. Parents and children are altruistically linked, with the former spending substantial resources to aid and support the latter, as well as (in some cases) leaving bequests. Children in their turn may end up supporting their parents in old age.

In theory, therefore, any intergenerational transfers within a given household at the government's behest can be reversed by adjustments to other transfers within the household. For example, parents might leave their children larger bequests by reason of government debts that the parents realize will have to be repaid. Or children might not gain from reducing their parents' Medicare coverage and thus their own taxes, because they would end up paying for the parents' healthcare anyway.

Among economists, the view that the government's generational policy is therefore irrelevant goes by the name of Ricardianism, in tribute to an early (albeit skeptical) discussion by the great nineteenth-century English economist David Ricardo. The view has not, however, fared well in the recent literature, either theoretically or empirically. From a theoretical standpoint, even if we assume that people engage in rational, consistent, and well-informed long-term planning, Ricardianism holds only insofar as transfers within the household reflect pure altruism, in the sense of precisely equating one's own subjective well-being with that of one's parents and children. Notions of accidental bequest, strategic interaction between family members, and selective or situational altruism within the household suggest that the government's generational policy *will* make a difference (Shaviro 1997, 68–78). Empirical research confirms that Ricardian offsets to the government's generational policy are fairly limited (Altonji, Hayashi, and Kotlikoff 1992)—although Medicare policy may be more Ricardian than most if children would otherwise frequently pay for their parents' healthcare.

Accordingly, the government's generational policy, including that through Medicare, affects bottom-line distributional outcomes. We therefore should consider the merits, from a social insurance standpoint, of transferring wealth from younger to older generations. The issue is quite ambiguous. An initial point of interest is that the United States has for many decades been growing ever wealthier (periodic business cycle downturns aside). Worker productivity and real per capita gross domestic product (GDP) have been steadily on the rise. If this technology-driven trend continues, each succeeding generation will continue to be wealthier on a lifetime basis than the one before. Medicare's generational redistribution therefore is progressive, transferring money to groups that have less and thus might be presumed (all else equal) to value a marginal dollar more.

Now, however, suppose we enrich our comparison of the circumstances faced by different generations. A narrowly monetary measure such as GDP is misleading, not just because money isn't everything, but because (standing alone) it isn't anything. It is only worth what it can be used to buy, which has changed over time for technological and other reasons. Given the pace of technological advance since the birth of Medicare's first enrollee generations, the increase in real per capita GDP may actually understate the real improvement in material conditions. To be sure, various disamenities that GDP ignores, such as pollution and overcrowded highways, may have worsened during this time. On the positive side of the ledger, however, GDP includes goods and services at their market prices without regard to consumer surplus, which is the greater amount that one would pay for them if necessary, and that our forebears might have been willing to pay had the items been available then.

Consider electrification and the spread of car and air travel in the first half of the twentieth century, followed more recently by gadgets ranging from personal computers to cellular phones to DVD players to microwave ovens. Or consider that millions of people still live who were born at a time when penicillin had not yet been introduced, and pneumonia was known as the "old person's friend." Life expectancy has been increasing for decades and is expected to continue doing so. The amount that we would be willing to pay for antibiotics to cure pneumonia, and that people for centuries would have been willing to pay, surely is far greater than its cost.

From an egalitarian perspective, if GDP understates the real improvement over time in material conditions, Medicare's generational transfer policy may look better still. There is also an opposing consideration, however. If money can buy ever better things as time passes, then people who live later might value a marginal dollar more than their precursors, even though they are better off. Suppose that you could give a million dollars to either of two individuals who suffer from advanced colon cancer: one living in 2005 who cannot be helped, or one living in 2045 who can actually, at great expense, be cured. From a behind-the-veil standpoint, it is hard to argue against giving the money to the latter individual, even if she is better-off.

Healthcare expenses of the sort that Medicare covers present an intuitively compelling case for favoring later over earlier generations even if per capita wealth increases, since treatment options are continually improving. The implication is that we might choose behind the veil to transfer resources from worse-off people (ourselves) to better-off people in the future who could use the money to greater effect.

Redistribution between High-Earners and Low-Earners. Redistribution from high-earners to low-earners is straightforward social insurance against income risk, desirable up to a point notwithstanding moral hazard. As we saw in chapter 3, however, Medicare contributes little if anything to such transfers.

While worth knowing about, Medicare's lack of significant redistribution between high- and low-earners is not necessarily cause for concern. Given the variety of available tools for such redistribution, including the income tax and income-related transfer systems, one should start out by being agnostic about the need for Medicare to play a significant role here. (In the generational setting, by contrast, Medicare's age-dependent application causes it, along with Social Security, to stand out as a primary redistributive tool.) Issues of political economy, concerning how the use of Medicare seems likely to affect the political equilibrium regarding progressivity, are likely to be crucial to the assessment of what role it should play.

Household Redistribution to One-Earner Married Couples from Single Individuals and Two-Earner Couples. Medicare's redistribution to one-earner married couples is hard to rationalize in social insurance terms. Consider first the transfer from single individuals. Admittedly, a household of two (whether or not both work) has greater retirement needs than a household of one, just as it has greater pre-retirement needs. Notwithstanding the old adage that two can live as cheaply as one, each member of a household needs clothing and healthcare, and each must eat. Even economies of scale, such as in the living space needed to be reasonably comfortable, imply only that the larger household's needs are less per person, not that they are less overall.

But in addition to having greater needs than a household of one, a household of two adults also has greater resources, in the form of an extra pair of hands that it can use in meeting those needs. While this is perhaps most obvious if both spouses work in the labor market for a wage, it remains true if one of them stays home. Self-performed housework, no less than market work, is a form of economic production on behalf of all members of the household. It provides consumption benefits that otherwise would have to be paid for or forgone.

Even more clearly, one-earner couples are not necessarily worse-off than two-earner couples that have greater household income due to the secondary earner. Suppose that two households have the same economic opportunities, but that in one the wife stays home while in the other she works. If each household has chosen the course that its members consider best, one has no basis for concluding that the second household is better-off. This would imply that the people in the first household made the wrong decision from the standpoint of their own self-interest, which might be the case but would require further inquiry.

In sum, therefore, it is one thing to say that we should want retirement health insurance to cover nonworking spouses, but entirely another to say that the coverage should be funded by a transfer from other households. One could instead require one-earner households to pay more for the extra coverage they get—just as two-earner households do through the income and payroll taxes on both spouses' earnings. The main real-world political reason for Medicare's transfer to one-earner households may simply be that people have not thought about the system in this way. Both the lack of a direct connection between Medicare taxes and benefits and the fact that the fiscal system generally (in part for administrative reasons) ignores imputed income, such as that from self-performed housework, makes the oversight unsurprising.

If Medicare were the only source of undue transfers to one-earner couples, there might be little cause for concern. However, the rest of the fiscal system is similarly biased. In particular, the income tax and Social Security have the same bias as Medicare (Shaviro 2000a, 18, 57).

Regional Redistribution. Medicare's redistribution from regions where healthcare is relatively cheap, such as Minneapolis, to those where it is relatively costly, such as Miami, mainly presents issues of healthcare adequacy and efficiency (as I discussed in chapter 3). However, it may also to some extent raise distributional issues. Suppose, for example, that healthcare (like air conditioning) is inherently costlier in Miami than Minneapolis, perhaps reflecting wage or cost-of-living differences. Or suppose that people tend to sort themselves between the two cities based, among other factors, on their taste for more intensive versus more limited medical interventions when they are sick.

In either case, one might be able to offer some defense of Medicare's distributional effects. One could argue, for example, that expensive tastes, such as for more intensive healthcare or enjoying the amenities that may underlie a high cost of living, are evidence of valuing money a bit more. Yet there is a moral hazard problem when those who satisfy such tastes do not bear the cost. We do not generally base transfers on regionally associated taste differences, such as by paying for heat in Minnesota or air conditioning in Miami. It is unclear why the taste differences that might be at issue here should be treated more favorably.

Health-Based Redistribution. Medicare induces health-based redistribution from both the low-risk to the high-risk going in, and from the healthy to the sick as events play out. Both redistributions are easy to rationalize. They transfer money from the better-off to the worse-off (all else equal) under circumstances where it seems reasonable to surmise that the latter need the money more. In addition, some risk-based differences, such as the genetic, do not raise moral hazard issues because they are beyond the individual's control, and yet become uninsurable once known.

Transfers that can be affected by the enrollee's behavior, however, such as through diet, exercise, or seeking early preventive treatment, present moral hazard problems that Medicare does little to address. This point can be demonstrated by comparing Medicare's health-based redistribution to the ability-based redistribution of a Mirrleesean income tax. In the Mirrlees framework, desirable redistribution is limited by the fact that only earnings can be observed, whereas ability is the underlying distributional metric. Earnings are a signal of ability, but an imperfect one since they also reflect work effort. As the marginal tax rate (MTR) on earnings rises, the discouraging effect on work effort rises more than proportionately. Double the MTR, for example, and you may quadruple the labor supply distortion (Rosen 1999, 294). In optimal income tax models that apply this framework, while findings can vary substantially with assumptions about labor supply elasticity and declining marginal utility, as well as with the normative framework (such as utilitarianism or egalitarian welfarism), optimal MTRs often do not much exceed the 30 percent range (320–21).

Applying this framework to Medicare considered purely as a system of health-based redistribution, we might (following Bradford and Shaviro 2000) make the following substitutions:

• Health condition for ability, although health condition might be defined in terms either of physical well-being or capacity to be helped by medical treatment;

• Medical expenditure for earnings, as a signal of health condition (in lieu of ability) that is flawed by its also reflecting the extent to which one seeks care (the analogue to work effort);

• Medicare's marginal reimbursement rate (MRR) for the income tax's MTR (ignoring for simplicity the fact that Medicare payments are generally made directly to the healthcare provider, rather than to the patient as reimbursement). Thus, just as a 60 percent income tax MTR would mean that you pay 60 cents and keep 40 cents out of your next dollar of earnings, a 60 percent Medicare MRR would mean that you get reimbursed 60 cents and have to pay 40 cents out of your next dollar of medical expenditure.

At first glance, MTRs and MRRs may look like opposites. The higher the MTR, the more you pay the government, whereas the higher the MRR, the more the government pays you. However, a high MTR and a high MRR have in common the effect of dampening your economic incentives—to earn money in the case of the MTR, and to minimize expenditure in the case of the MRR. Accordingly, they are conceptually parallel despite involving opposite directions of cash flow.

Under this structure, what should we think of a system that, like Medicare's Part B coverage for outpatient services, has an 80 percent MRR that Medigap coverage can raise to 100 percent? Analogy to the income tax can suggest that the glass is either half-full or half-empty. On the one hand, the resulting distortions may be less than under an income tax with MTRs in the 80 percent to 100 percent range. As noted in chapter 3, in the RAND study of medical expenditure, as the MRR fell from 100 percent to 5 percent, annual per-person expenditure declined by about 30 percent (Newhouse et al. 1993, 79). An income tax MTR of 80 to 100 percent—if people actually had to pay it despite tax planning—might have significantly greater incentive-based effects on work effort.

But turning from the half-full to the half-empty aspect, the RAND study suggests enough price sensitivity to imply that Medicare's high MRRs lead to waste and adverse budgetary effects, possibly in the tens of billions of dollars per year. Recall as well that the study found no discernible adverse health impact from decreasing MRRs except among the sick poor (339), who may have Medicaid coverage whether or not they are enrolled in Medicare. Accordingly, if we look at Medicare purely as redistribution from the healthy to the sick, it appears to over-reimburse routine expenditures, given the limited character of the insurance benefits.

Turning to Medicare MRRs at very high expenditure levels, the ceiling on Part A coverage and lack of a ceiling on Part B copayments cause seniors to lack catastrophic protection, unless it is provided by their Medigap plans. (Medicaid may step in, but only after the patient's assets have been depleted.) Private insurance plans, by contrast, frequently have a stop-loss provision under which the MRR ultimately rises to 100 percent, for outpatient or Part B–type services as well as hospitalization. This dispensing with coinsurance presumably reflects consumers' high demand for limiting the risk of financial wipeout, along with the relative ease of monitoring a rare and extreme situation.

Assessing Medicare's National Healthcare Plan as a Social Insurance and Risk Prevention System

Reasons for In-Kind Benefits

Suppose people were offered Medicare buy-outs in the form of cash equaling the present value of all its remaining actuarially expected payments on their behalf. Absent paternalism and externalities, this buy-out option would increase the welfare of those who were offered it while leaving the taxpayers' position unchanged. With those two motivations, however, Medicare's in-kind character is easy to rationalize.

There may also be a distributional reason for the in-kind benefits. Suppose we want to redistribute from the healthy to the sick, and that medical expenditures are easier to monitor than health status. Then the noncash character of the benefits may simply reflect a trade-off between administrative cost-saving in identifying the sick and the waste from providing benefits that are worth less to the recipient than their cost.

Mandatory Retirement Health Insurance

The paternalist ground for requiring that Medicare enrollees take B in the form of health insurance is clearcut. Such insurance seems well worth having, since it helps allocate extra dollars to states of the world where you will need them more. Yet people often underappreciate the benefit of hedging risks (Shiller 1993, 17), and think of insurance as valueless in cases where they did not collect on it.

The intangible character of insurance may limit the extent to which, by supplying it, Medicare directly addresses an altruistic externality. Giving someone insurance that she would otherwise lack does not fire the imagination in quite the same way as giving her food when she is hungry. Given, however, that people who lack health insurance coverage may nonetheless receive treatment when they need it, with the cost presumably being passed on to healthcare consumers generally, lack of insurance creates a straightforward financial externality that we might want to limit by making coverage mandatory (Coate 1995).

These arguments for mandatory health insurance, which lie more in the realm of preventing risk than risk-spreading, help to answer the question of why we cannot simply rely on private markets to furnish health insurance to enrollees. However, they may not greatly alter the distribution-based analysis of optimal MRRs. Paternalist arguments presumably imply mandating well-designed insurance, rather than that which provides substantial first-dollar coverage for routine expenses but only limited high-end coverage. Likewise, concern about the financial externality supports requiring people to invest a part of B in paying for high-end coverage that might otherwise end up getting passed on to taxpayers through Medicaid or to healthcare consumers generally.

Paying Healthcare Expenses of the Elderly

When we look at national healthcare in the sense of paying medical expenses as they arise, the paternalist case for offering B in-kind plays a lesser role. What makes paternalism plausible in the various settings discussed above is the notion that people have difficulty in dealing with time and with uncertainty. However, most people presumably know best how they feel and what they want now. Thus, the altruistic externality does most of the work here. Voters presumably sympathize with seniors who have healthcare needs. Even if these seniors would rationally prefer other consumption goods, the voters might get less satisfaction that way.

The altruistic externality may increase optimal MRRs, because moral hazard in choosing healthcare may function like an efficient subsidy. Suppose a given senior is considering an outpatient procedure that costs $100 and is valued by her at $20. If we were to imagine an altruistic externality from the treatment of exactly $80, then the 80 percent MRR in Part B of

Medicare would fortuitously give her exactly the right incentive in comparing cost and benefit.

Still, the altruistic externality does not imply high MRRs in all settings. Healthcare altruists presumably value the end result of improving seniors' health, as distinct from the delivery of healthcare services as an end in itself. Moreover, people may attach little or no value to providing healthcare in excess of what they define as an adequate level (Feldstein 1998, 516). Medicare may therefore oversubsidize services that convey little medical benefit, even considering the altruistic externality.

Summary

Government intervention can often be justified as expanding choice by offering goods that private markets are unable to supply. An example is income insurance, which is subject to adverse selection if privately offered. Governments can require residents to participate in an income tax and income-conditioned welfare system. Alternatively, government intervention can be justified as limiting consumer choice, on paternalistic grounds or in response to externalities.

Medicare's first two subprograms, pertaining to forced saving and portfolio choice, are examples of limiting choice. They can be justified in terms of both paternalism (lifecycle saving and rational portfolio choice) and externalities (voters' preference for healthcare consumption by seniors). These subprograms do, however, have design flaws. In particular, the forced saving subprogram limits the extent to which costly technological advances in healthcare induce increased national saving. Under Medicare, the extra costs are "financed" through an implicit increase in the expected transfer from future generations to current ones.

Medicare's redistributive subprogram looks more like a response to straight market failure. Again, however, various of the details can be criticized. Its poorly understood lack of progressivity may affect overall distributional outcomes. Its wealth transfer from the young to the old is probably progressive, but shifts resources to generations that cannot use the money as well. The transfers to one-earner couples are hard to rationalize.

Medicare's subprograms to provide health insurance and actual healthcare make sense in terms of paternalism and externalities, in addition to serving a redistributive rationale as between the healthy and the sick. However, the MRRs are probably too high for routine expenditures and too low at the high end.

Medicare's Long-Term Fiscal Gap and
Its Underlying Causes

Despite any possible criticism of Medicare's current structure, the only reason Medicare reform, apart from just adding new unfunded benefits, is even on the table politically is that the program has a projected long-term fiscal gap. This, so far, is merely a statement about perceptions and politics: whether or not the fiscal gap actually matters, people think it does. It has actual substance as well, however.

To grasp this underlying substance, we need to proceed in a couple of stages. This chapter discusses the magnitude and reasons for the Medicare fiscal gap. Chapter 7 considers the broader fiscal picture, and the significance of an overall fiscal gap.

Magnitude of the Medicare Fiscal Gap

Medicare's 2001 expenditures of $244.8 billion represented 2.4 percent of gross domestic product (GDP) for the year. Over time, however, its expenditures are projected to grow much faster than the economy. Under the official intermediate estimates, they will reach 5 percent of GDP by 2035 and 8.6 percent by 2075, approaching a fourfold relative increase (Boards of Trustees 2002, 2–3).

There are two main reasons for this relative growth. First, Medicare's demographic balance is changing for the worse. Its current ratio of four workers per Part A enrollee is expected to decline by half before 2076, and then to continue declining as life expectancies remain on an upward course (18). Second, and even more significantly (Fuchs 2000, 16), Medicare expenditures per enrollee, reflecting a general trend in the healthcare sector of the economy, are expected to grow 1 percent faster than GDP (Boards of Trustees 2002, 6). This trend has been mainly technology-driven. Over the last thirty years, for example, "[e]xpenditures grew primarily because the medical care system was delivering more and better services to patients: new drugs, MRIs, angioplasties, hip replacements, and many other costly interventions. Advances in medical technology have made it feasible and desirable to do more for each patient and to intervene with more patients" (Fuchs 1998b, 2).

By reason of the changes in life expectancy and medical technology, the apex of the pyramid is both widening relative to the base and growing heavier per square inch. Medicare's revenue sources do not automatically adjust for the projected expenditure growth. Revenues from the Medicare portion of the payroll tax, if it continues to be a flat 2.9 percent levy, should grow roughly proportionately to GDP. Income tax revenues may grow a bit faster, since the income tax has graduated rates with brackets that are indexed just for inflation, not for economic growth. Yet the difference is not all that great. Finally, rising Part B premiums keep pace with one-quarter of the growth in Part B expenditure, but do nothing to help with the rest.

Suppose that Medicare were operated on a strict annual pay-as-you-go basis, so that each year's dedicated tax revenues had to equal expenditures. Then, while the current Part A tax rate would only be 2.75 percent, by 2075 it would have to be 10.61 percent (60). Meanwhile, by 2075, Part B would be commandeering 22.8 percent, rather than the current 6 percent, of individual plus corporate income tax revenues (96).

Near-quadrupling of Medicare tax rates (including the implicit Medicare portion of the income tax) is not necessary, of course, if we start restoring the program's long-term fiscal solvency immediately. This might involve increasing Medicare's taxes relative to its expenditures without effectively dissipating the buildup through tax cuts or spending increases in the rest of the federal budget. According to Medicare's trustees, however, restoring seventy-five-year balance in Part A—while ignoring the ever-widening shortfall from year 76 on—would require immediately reducing outlays by 38 percent, increasing revenues by 60 percent, or some combination of the two (3). Part B does not have a similarly explicit long-term balance requirement since it is funded by general revenues, but over the seventy-five-year period its expenditures are projected to grow even faster than those in Part A, so the implications are worse despite the lack of an insolvency trigger mechanism.

Economists David Cutler and Louise Sheiner (2000, 306) reach similar conclusions about Medicare's long-term finances. They estimate that permanently restoring the program's long-term fiscal balance would require immediate benefit cuts of 38–61 percent. Or, if handled entirely on the tax side, assuming for simplicity that the Medicare payroll tax did all of the work, its rate would have to rise from 2.9 percent to at least 7 percent, and perhaps to as much as 12.3 percent.

Even in combination, any of these would be huge changes, going well beyond what anyone today thinks is politically tolerable. Hence, Medicare's current policy path is unsustainable, leaving aside for now the question of whether general revenues under current policy could make up the difference. Closing the Medicare fiscal gap would appear to be impossible under all real-world policy options that voters might at present consider acceptable.

Medicare's Structure as a Non-prefunded Defined Benefit Plan

Shrinking worker to retiree ratios and rising healthcare expenditures relative to GDP would stress any effort, whether managed by the government or the private sector, to provide adequate healthcare to retirees. Yet Medicare is not just a fortuitous victim of these trends. Certain of its basic structural elements, dating back to its enactment, have helped to shape the manner in which the stresses have played out.

In particular, Medicare would not be facing a fiscal crisis—although it might instead be facing an adequacy-of-benefits crisis—if not for two key elements in its structure. The first is that it is a defined-benefit (DB) plan that purports to make outright commitments to provide certain healthcare to retirees, rather than a defined-contribution (DC) plan that conditions benefit levels on available, set-aside funds. DC plans are inherently self-financing, although they can lead to disappointment regarding the benefits that end up being available.

Second, unlike a classic private-sector DB plan, Medicare has been operated on more of a pay-as-you-go than a prefunded basis. And even such prefunding as there has been (since Part A's historical revenues have exceeded its expenditures) has not been of the straightforward and conservative kind best suited to ensure long-term funding adequacy. In the typical private-sector DB plan, the people who are actually going to get the benefits pay for them first, at least in actuarially expected terms. While the primary reason for this is the difficulty of running a transfer program through voluntary employment arrangements (since the losers could simply opt out), it also makes the achievement of funding adequacy a simpler proposition. First you pay, then the funds you have contributed grow, and finally down the road you get what you have paid for—although the DB structure may require adjusting your payments as time goes by to meet new information about their adequacy.

There are several reasons, however, why neither a DC plan, nor a fully funded DB plan, nor indeed any plan where people pay in advance for their own benefits has much appeal either as a matter of crass politics or even in genuine substance. It is therefore no coincidence that government retirement plans around the world, including Social Security in the United

States, generally share with Medicare the structural features that have recently led to severe long-term financing problems. In particular:

• Self-funding, and any conservative approach to prefunding, may require a considerable time lag between when a program is announced and when it actually starts delivering benefits. Imagine the sense of anticlimax if President Johnson, when proposing Medicare in 1965, had said: "I have a great idea, which taxpayers should start paying for immediately, but which will not actually start helping anyone for (say) twenty years."

• Even if such a proposal were politically realistic, it would properly raise concern about the political risk of having the government sit on a substantial pile of cash that was not immediately being used. Who would decide how it was invested? How could one be sure that greedy hands would not find a more immediate use for it? The government's very strength is in a sense its weakness. Its power to change the laws at any time makes credible precommitment, of the sort available to a private firm by placing funds in trust or escrow, hard to achieve.

• Suppose that concern about contemporaneous seniors motivates adoption of the program, as was the case in both 1935 (for Social Security) and 1965 (for Medicare). Waiting for the funds to build up, and asking people to pay for their own benefits once they are past their working years, would mean that nothing could be done for them.

Retirement plans without prefunding, and in which the members of the first generation of enrollees get benefits for free, may therefore be politically inevitable and also serve good purposes. Moreover, such plans need not, at least as a matter of logical compulsion, prove fiscally unsustainable over time. Indeed, this is so even if the transfer to the first generation is indefinitely carried forward, rather than being definitively repaid in the transition to a system where people pay in advance for their own benefits.

One example of a non-prefunded plan where the first generation gets benefits for free, and which might in theory be sustainable indefinitely, is a Ponzi scheme. Consider an (illegal) chain letter in which the originator solicits eight people to send her a dollar apiece and each then solicits eight more people to send her a dollar apiece, going forward indefinitely. There is no specific point at which such a scheme must fall apart (leaving losers at the end of the chain to balance the winners up front), so long as members of the population are willing to be repeat players an unlimited number of times.

To be sure, even if a Ponzi scheme is not logically compelled to fail at some specific point (or ever), its "exploding" character—the fact that its participants and cash flows grow exponentially—makes it especially subject to rapid collapse. Non-prefunded programs need not be designed to explode like this, however. We therefore need to consider a more benign and sustainable type of non-prefunded, immediate-gratification plan, drawing on economics literature about Social Security that is readily applicable (though to my knowledge it has not yet been applied) to Medicare.

The Samuelson Model of Social Security and Its Applicability to Medicare

Description of the Samuelson Model

Paul Samuelson (1958) famously proposed a nonexploding cousin of Ponzi schemes to explain and justify Social Security. Despite its extreme abstraction, his model merits attention with regard to Medicare as well. Samuelson brilliantly succeeded in capturing some of the basic elements of both programs in a fashion that helps us to explore their appeal and potential feasibility.

Samuelson's basic idea can be explained as follows. Suppose initially, for simplicity, that each age cohort consists of the same number of individuals. Everyone lives for two equal periods: a work period and a retirement period. The society's demographics are therefore fixed: neither birth levels nor life expectancies ever change. In this society, suppose that saving, including for retirement, is for some reason impossible (for example, all physical assets disintegrate each day at sundown, and financial assets such as money do not exist). Absurd though this assumption might seem, it is not a bad approximation of how things looked in the 1930s, when economic growth was actually negative and the banking system was teetering near collapse. Even past the 1930s, the underlying problem captured by the assumption might be that people do not save enough and cannot be directly forced to do so. Thus, they act as if adequate saving were impossible. Or instead, as Henry Aaron (1966) posited, the underlying motivation for Samuelson's model might be that the interest rate on saving lies perpetually below the rate of productivity growth in the workforce.

Under these circumstances, Samuelson pointed out, the workers of all generations might benefit from the adoption of the following program. The members of Generation 1 (retirees when the program is adopted) are supported at retirement by the proceeds of a permanently fixed, flat-rate payroll tax that first applies to the members of Generation 2. Those individuals, in turn, are supported at retirement by the proceeds from levying this tax on the members of Generation 3, and so on going forward indefinitely. So long as workers' earnings (which make up the tax base) continually grow, each taxpaying generation ends up getting back more than it put in. Since workers are paid for the value of what they produce, these earnings increase over time at the rate of productivity growth.

Medicare did not yet exist in 1958, and Samuelson therefore did not consider applying his model to it. It is easy enough for us to do so, however. All we need add is the proviso that a slice of the payroll tax revenues are used to provide healthcare benefits to retirees.

The Samuelson model's appeal lies in the idea that despite its (seemingly imprudently) giving the first generation benefits for free, it might not only be indefinitely sustainable but leave all generations better off than if it did not exist. Generation 1, to be sure, fares the best under it, by getting retirement support for free. So long as the program keeps going, however, each subsequent generation wins as well. Suppose, for example, that, absent the program, the members of Generation 2 would have (or at least should have) saved the same amount as their payroll taxes to help pay for their retirement. In the Aaron variant, the program enables them to increase their return on this saving from the interest rate that they would have earned on their own to the rate of productivity growth.[1]

Now suppose that, like Samuelson (1958, 471–74) in his original article, we relax the assumption that population size is fixed, and contemplate as well the possibility of population growth. The result is to make things better still. Now, if X is the percentage by which the worker generation is more numerous than the retiree generation due to population growth, each retiree is being supported by the payroll taxes on one plus X workers, rather than just by one worker. Accordingly, population growth joins productivity growth as a source of positive returns to each generation on the amount it notionally invested in the program by paying payroll taxes. So each generation ends up even better-off than it would have been with population size fixed.

To be sure, in order to accept that all generations win from the program, you may need to keep on reminding yourself of the underlying assumption that there is no last generation that would pay for its predecessors' benefits, yet never get paid back. Samuelson (1958, 480 n. 19) dismissed any concern that "the final young will be cheated by the demise of the human race" by asking: "Should such a cheating of one generation 30 million years from now perpetually condemn society to a suboptimal configuration?"

To this one might reply: "Doesn't it depend on which generation we ask?" (And 30 million years sounds a bit optimistic anyway.) Perhaps, however, any unease about this possibility can be shrugged off on the ground that whatever events make a given generation the last (nuclear war? environmental collapse?) might also eliminate their need for retirement saving. Yet population shrinkage—a lesser case of the last-generation scenario—is not quite so easily shrugged off, unlikely though it may have seemed back in 1958. Samuelson wrote before various industrialized countries began experiencing birth rates that were below long-term population replacement levels.

In addition to giving everyone until the end a better return than would otherwise have been available, the Samuelson model serves desirable risk-spreading or social insurance purposes. The better-off the new generation of workers is (that is, the greater their earnings given productivity growth), and thus the more it can afford to pay, the more it ends up paying. Retirees share in both upturns and downturns relative to the mean expected rate of productivity growth. Absent the program, this set of risks might have ended up being borne by the workers alone.

Yet, no matter how good the Samuelson model looks on paper, the question of real importance is how much it tells us about the real world. This depends on the empirical accuracy and applicability of its underlying assumptions. As it turns out, even as applied to Social Security, real-world conditions may cause the model to have perverse distributional results and face a risk of collapse that Samuelson did not anticipate. Applying it to Medicare further adds to the problems.

This should not be taken as criticism of Paul Samuelson, a giant of modern economics who, through a leap of imagination, jump-started serious academic writing about age-related social insurance systems. We should all be so lucky as to develop seminal ideas that are worth the effort of sustained criticism more than forty years later. Yet the problems with his model, as we now can understand them, are worth exploring.

Demographic "Bad Luck"

The Achilles heel of the Samuelson model, as applied to both Social Security and Medicare, is its assuming demographics that are either fixed or favorable. Under the model, each generation has at least the same number of individuals as the preceding generation, and the members of each generation live for the same fixed retirement period. Thus, no demographic "noise" can disrupt the relationship between productivity growth and the average rate of return to the members of each generation, except in a favorable direction in the case of population growth.

In the real world, things are not so simple. The more obvious point is that, in the last few decades, the enormous "baby boom" that was ongoing when Samuelson wrote has been followed by a relative "baby bust." In addition, life expectancies have increased by 10 percent in just the last forty years (Lichtenberg 2000) and are expected to continue rising. The result of these shifts is ineluctable demographic risk that includes a downside as well as an upside.

While demographic risk could be allocated in multiple ways, perhaps it is most illuminating to consider a DB system—like Social Security and Medicare although unlike the DC-style Samuelson model—that operates on a pure pay-as-you-go basis (that is, revenues equal expenditures each year). In such a system, a worker generation wins when it is more numerous than the retiree generation it supports, since this permits a lower payroll tax to meet the desired support level. But the worker generation loses when it is less numerous than retirees, and thus must pay a higher payroll tax to reach the support level that has been promised.

Changes in life expectancy have a similar destabilizing effect. Workers lose when the retirees they are supporting live longer, and win when the reverse happens. At least, this is clear under Social Security, since it offers a fixed real annuity to retirees while they live. Medicare is similar, since it offers a fixed set of annual health insurance benefits to those who remain alive, although here the impact of life expectancy changes may be ambiguous. Longer-lived individuals presumably are healthier in early retirement than those who are closer to death, and thus may conceivably require less medical expenditure, at least for a while.

The distributional effects of demographic "bad luck" tend to be perverse. Again, under the pure Samuelson DC model, the fact that the level of retirement support varies with how well the worker generation is doing serves desirable risk-spreading or social insurance features. It is hard to come up with similar reasoning in support of having the average return to members of a given generation depend on the relative size of other generations. After all, unless there is more to the story, the number of people in different age groups has little to do with their relative well-being or need. Only if transfers under the Samuelson model offset some naturally occurring economic by-product of changing generational size should we applaud the risk-sharing properties.

Unfortunately, the opposite effect—accentuating the risks associated with generation size—seems more plausible. In particular, small generations may tend to win, and large generations to lose, in economic exchanges outside as well as inside Social Security and Medicare. Workers offer services to retirees at wages that reflect supply and demand. The greater the number of workers compared to retirees, the lower the equilibrium wage for those services will presumably be. Being in a large generation that is transacting with a small generation means that you have more trade competitors and fewer trading partners.[2]

Now suppose that the members of this same large generation, upon retirement, must sell their homes, along with investment assets that they liquidate to pay for retirement, to a small succeeding generation of workers. Again, being in a large generation worsens the terms of exchange for members of the group. This is why some predict that today's baby boomers will face falling prices when they start en masse selling their homes and liquidating their stock portfolios at retirement. Thus, if Social Security and Medicare benefit members of small generations relative to large ones, the programs operate in precisely the wrong direction from the standpoint of spreading demographic risk.

To be sure, such risk is unavoidable in the real world. Neither the Samuelson model, nor actual Social Security and Medicare, can reasonably be blamed for it, or expected to offer a perfect solution. What is more, once we relax Samuelson's assumptions so that saving is possible (even if it earns less than the rate of productivity growth), the question of how we ought to deal with demographic risk is just one more challenge for the analysis. For example, we might improve the system by allowing large generations to devote a portion of their payroll taxes to saving for their own retirement. Or we might use debt financing to pay for some of their benefits when they retire, counting on large future generations to pay off the debt.

From a practical political standpoint, however, the question is not just whether such responses are theoretically possible. Will they in fact be chosen? After all, if each generation is to some extent self-interested, then its aim when at the political controls will be to maximize its own gain from the system rather than to optimize distributional outcomes in light of everyone's interests.

Such political risk may pose a problem, of course, even in the basic Samuelson model without demographic risk. Samuelson, however, thought he had solved it within the contours of his model (most notably, a perpetually fixed payroll tax) that constant or favorable demographics made possible. All that the members of each generation would need to decide, he posited, was whether to agree as workers to fulfill the payroll tax obligation that their elders had placed on them. They would realize, however, that, if they reneged, the next generation would not pay them, whereas if they met their obligation then the next generation would face the same choice that they now did.

If saving were literally impossible (as in the pure Samuelson model), then the workers' only chance to survive as retirees would be to have the next generation agree to support them. Even under the Aaron variant, where the interest rate on saving is below the rate of productivity growth, they would realize that dedicating the payroll taxes to their own retirement rather than to supporting their elders would leave them worse-off than if they met their obligation and the next generation did, too.

"[H]ow easy it is," Samuelson concluded, "to get to the optimum" under such circumstances. "Let mankind enter into a Hobbes-Rousseau social contract in which the young are assured of their retirement subsistence if they will today support the aged, such support to be guaranteed by a draft on the yet-unborn. . . . [T]he young never suffer, since their successors come under the same requirement. Everybody ends up better off. It is as simple as that" (479–80).

Alas, it is not as simple as that if the program needs periodic adjustment in response to demographic shocks. Deciding how to respond to these shocks is considerably more discretionary than just going along with a fixed program in place. As soon as demographic risk requires or invites tinkering with the system's parameters, the self-interest problem is back in full force. Moreover, it is not as simple as that if retirees have the political power to increase their benefits under the program, having already completed the stage where their own contribution as workers was determined. Finally, it is not as simple as that if the political system is prone to reacting quite slowly, in particular to demographic "bad news" that jeopardizes the long-term sustainability of Social Security and Medicare.

In recent decades, adverse demographic trends—the baby boom followed by the baby bust, but more importantly, the steady increase in life expectancies—have combined to put Medicare, as well as Social Security, in grave long-term fiscal condition. (Increasing life expectancies is really a good thing, of course, but fiscally speaking is adverse.) Future generations, which have the most to gain from immediate adjustments to the programs, have no current political voice. Seniors, who have the most to lose from such adjustments, are politically the strongest.

Thus, the demographic trends, given the politics, have helped to move both Medicare and Social Security much closer to Ponzi territory than one might have expected from the seemingly nonexploding character of the Samuelson model. We now understand that, given current voters' incentives, non-prefunded retirement programs are quite likely to experience fiscal distress, as they recently have around the world, when life expectancies are lengthening and baby boom generations are heading toward the retirement segment of their lives.

Healthcare Expenditure Growth

Considered as a Samuelson-style program, Medicare faces a second type of risk from which Social Security is exempt. It places a bet not just on demographic trends, but also on the growth of healthcare expenditure relative to the overall economy. After all, Medicare outlays depend on how much seniors spend on covered healthcare.

If Medicare were a DC plan like the Samuelson model, retirees might be the ones bearing the risk that, over time, the cost of their healthcare would increase at a different rate than the wage base. Suppose, for example, that at retirement a fixed-rate payroll tax would be used to offer them vouchers that they could use toward purchasing private-sector health insurance coverage. If healthcare costs increased relative to the wage base, the cost of insurance, which must on average meet these costs, presumably would increase commensurately. Retirees would therefore find that the coverage they could purchase using the vouchers was shrinking relative to the total healthcare that (given available services) they might have liked to have.

To be sure, so long as economic growth was positive, each year the vouchers would be purchasing more healthcare in real terms than they did the year before. Moreover, so long as any increase in healthcare costs reflected the introduction of new and improved treatments (the fruits of medical research) rather than price inflation, each year the vouchers would be purchasing better healthcare than they did the year before. Thus, Medicare's positive contribution to retirees' welfare would increase over time without regard to the relative growth rates. Retirees would nonetheless bear a very specific type of risk with regard to the relative growth rates. This would be the risk of wanting medical procedures that the vouchers were not high enough to cover, and thus that they might have to go without. Their out-of-pocket costs for such medical procedures would increase if healthcare costs grew more rapidly than the wage base, and would decline if the wage base grew faster.

All this, however, is under the counterfactual assumption of a DC plan. Once we recognize that Medicare is actually more of a DB plan, we can see that the risk pertaining to healthcare costs is mainly borne by workers. Their payroll taxes for Medicare will presumably have to respond to trends in program expenditure that reflect how healthcare costs are changing relative to the economy. This healthcare risk, like demographic risk, can in principle prompt ongoing adjustments to Medicare financing. For example, payroll taxes might be increased as soon as the likelihood of a relative increase in healthcare costs was detected. Once again, however, the need for ongoing adjustment complicates the political side by requiring voters to do more than just sign on to a fixed program.

Indeed, politics makes the risk asymmetric. Seniors' political power makes them more likely to win an expansion of Medicare coverage if healthcare costs shrink relative to the economy than to face a reduction in coverage if the relative costs increase. To similar effect is the influence of "an ideology that holds that benefits currently promised to the elderly can be increased but not reduced" (Shaviro 2000a, 71). We have recently seen this phenomenon operating in real time. The explosion of prescription drug costs led to a political consensus that unfunded coverage should be added to seniors' Medicare benefits (at least through managed care) despite the program's dire long-term fiscal projections. In short, the fact that seniors' uncovered healthcare costs were increasing proved to have vastly more political weight than the fact that present or future workers' burden to pay for covered costs was also increasing.

Now consider that healthcare costs have for many years been growing rapidly relative to the economy—a trend that many expect to continue indefinitely. Again, the main cause is new developments in medical technology that make possible costly treatments for medical conditions that previously could not be treated as effectively if at all (Glied 1997, 91). The result is that Medicare's long-term fiscal picture is considerably graver than Social Security's. So once again good news has bad fiscal consequences.

The problem of how to adjust for technological risk has no good solution. From the standpoint of incentives, we might want seniors, during their working years, to have borne the risk of costly medical advances that indicate they should save more. There are two problems with this, however. First, the future may simply be too hard to anticipate fully. Consider the first group of seniors to participate in Medicare when it was enacted. They had reached their forties by the time that penicillin became widely available, yet many of them lived well into the era of magnetic resonance imaging (MRIs) and prosthetic surgery. There is a limit to how much prescience one could realistically have expected from them.

Second, since future medical treatment options are radically uncertain, people who are risk averse should want to insure against the variance. A generation, however, has no counterparties who will be on hand when the uncertainty is resolved except for younger generations. Yet the latter will also want more resources if healthcare costs and options increase (although at least they are not past the point of saving for their own retirements). The insurance coverage therefore comes from people who bear the same risk, rather than from those with uncorrelated risks as in classic insurance.

Technology and Moral Hazard

A further problem arising from Medicare's DB character is that technological change may affect the moral hazard problem that arises when people's healthcare expenditures are subsidized. The basic problem could be understood by any parent who has given her teenagers credit cards. The higher the credit limit, the greater the financial damage the teenagers can inflict. For Medicare enrollees, new medical technology does the equivalent of raising the teenager's credit limit. New treatments present new opportunities to spend money, expanding what is actually available under the ostensibly DB plan. Thus, a Medicare marginal reimbursement rate (MRR) that was just right at one point in time might subsequently be too high.

In terms of the Samuelson model, the problem is a lack of political incentives to address this problem as it arises by adjusting MRRs. The burden of paying for a given generation's expanded healthcare opportunities therefore tends to be pushed forward to future generations. They, of course, will have their own still greater new healthcare spending opportunities, as technology advances and costly new treatments continue to emerge. Once again, the distributional effects seem perverse. All else equal, we may want to spend more on a given generation (despite moral hazard) because healthcare advances have given doctors the ability to do new things for them. Why not, for example, start spending more money on heart attack victims once the development of open heart surgery means that we can actually help them recover? If we look just at the present, this is exactly what Medicare does, and it may seem all to the good. Yet, by handing the bill to future generations, we burden people to whom the dollars we are taking might have been worth even more. Suppose, for example, that costly cancer cures or remediation of genetic defects emerge over the next few decades, just when payroll taxes have to be increased or Medicare has to be cut back.

Assessing the Blame for Medicare's Financing Problems: Demographics or Politics?

We can now better address an underlying causal question concerning Medicare's long-term financing problems, which is of interest less as an exercise in scapegoating than to help us down the road in evaluating realistic solutions. Is Medicare the long-run victim of inexorable demographic trends or of political failure? The answer lies in the interaction of the two, rather than either considered in isolation. For political reasons (including good policy reasons), Medicare was given a particular structure that made it subject to certain demographic and technological risks. Politics then impeded addressing the ill fruit of these risks in a timely or coherent fashion.

Yet it would be easy to exaggerate and misconstrue the political problems and their contribution to the fiscal gap. Richard Epstein (1999, 151–52) claims that Medicare as enacted "was laced with caveats and reeked prudence from every pore. But once in place, the program's scope could be expanded [repeatedly]. . . . [A]nd new expectations could lift Medicare to a near-sacred Social Compact between the generations. Just as water flows downhill, so power and rhetoric move inexorably in one direction only. Grand programs expand inexorably—until they crash." Similarly if more prosaically, Andrew Rettenmaier and Thomas Saving (1999, 184) complain of "Congress's penchant [for] subsidizing 'worthy' causes with any funds that appear available."

Now, clearly there is some content to this story. Congress has indeed on several occasions approved significant expansions of Medicare coverage without accompanying funding. Such changes have only been sporadic, however. And since the 1980s, Congress has repeatedly looked for ways to cut the Medicare budget, either as part of deficit reduction or so that the program will be more sustainable over time. An example is the adoption in the 1980s of new Part A and Part B price controls to cut the program's costs (Marmor 2000, 175).

However enjoyable as rhetoric, Epstein's account of a system that initially reeked of prudence and then inexorably grew besotted on the logic of expanding commitment does not fit the facts. Despite the instances of augmentation, "there has been no dramatic expansion of who is covered or for what medical costs" (Marmor 2000, 173). Indeed, Medicare's benefit coverage has failed to keep pace with the standard in the private insurance market (Oberlander 2003, 11). Thus, the chief problem is indeed that, with the benefit of hindsight, Medicare's Samuelson financing was unsustainable from the start, given the demographic and economic trends that emerged and the political system's inability to respond to them promptly.

The limits to Medicare's political expansion reflect that even the strongest interest groups are not all-powerful. The interest of the elderly in expanding or at least protecting Medicare rests in good part on the shoulders of the American Association of Retired Persons (AARP)—"by far the most powerful interest group on Capital Hill," and capable of inspiring a "fear level in Congress [that] is just incredible" (Vogel 1999, 128). Even the AARP, however, can only do so much. In blocking Medicare changes that are adverse to its members' interests, it is formidable indeed. Yet, even in seeking prescription drug coverage, which emerged as a key issue for seniors by the late 1980s, it could not just snap its fingers and immediately get what it wanted. There simply were too many rival claimants in Washington, either for center stage when only so many issues can grab Congress's attention, or for scarce government dollars. The AARP loses as well as wins from "demosclerosis" (Rauch 1994), or the difficulty of enacting any sort of major policy change when so many rival interests, each with significant veto power, are perennially at the ready to protect their existing turfs.

Summary

Medicare has a huge projected long-term fiscal gap. Over the next seventy-five years, its expenditures are expected to grow by 400 percent relative to the size of the economy, while its current revenue sources grow scarcely faster than the economy. Achieving long-term fiscal stability for Medicare might require changes on the order of an immediate 40 percent benefit cut or 60 percent expenditure increase—alternatives well outside the realm of political acceptability.

The projected fourfold expenditure growth has two main causes. The first is demographic: increasing life expectancies that require ever-longer periods of retirement health insurance for enrollees. The second is technological: increased healthcare expenditure relative to GDP, given the continuing development of new options for intensive treatment. This second problem interacts with the underlying incentive problem in health insurance (lack of cost consciousness by the consumer) by increasing the scale of the expenditures that could be sought.

These two "problems"—each actually a good thing from the broader societal standpoint—would pose a challenge for any public or private health insurance system. However, Medicare's particular fiscal problems reflect two key elements of its structure. The first is its being a nominally DB (defined-benefit) plan that offers a specific (but in practice technology-dependent) menu of benefits to enrollees. The second is its using the funding methodology described in the Samuelson model: free benefits for the first generation of enrollees, followed by financing that is closer to pay-as-you-go than to full prefunding and that relies on taxing current workers at a fixed rate. These features subject the program to demographic and economic risk that has borne fruit in the form of accelerating fiscal shortfalls.

In theory, adjustments can be made to the Samuelson model to handle these demographic and economic risks relatively smoothly. In practice, however, political actors lack the incentives to adjust Medicare's finances on a timely basis rather than simply deferring problems to the future. By contrast, under Samuelson's restrictive assumptions, the great beauty of the model had been that it appeared to solve political incentive problems by requiring each generation merely to accept an ongoing fixed program that was in their interest.

Significance of Medicare's Long-Term
Fiscal Gap

THE reasons for Medicare's looming fiscal gap might be
of intellectual interest even if they had no policy implications. Their normative significance, however, depends both on budgetary
trends outside Medicare, which help determine whether there is an overall
fiscal gap, and on the question of why a fiscal gap matters to begin with.

The Overall Fiscal Picture

Looking beyond Medicare

Suppose that only Medicare was in long-term deficit, while overall government revenues seemed likely over time to equal or exceed government
outlays without requiring any change to our projected tax and spending
policies. Then the Medicare fiscal gap would not be a major concern. One
therefore needs to consider the overall long-term fiscal picture.

Assessing this is no easy matter, however, for two kinds of reasons.
First, the future is hard to predict. Even if we can agree on a definition of
current policy over the long term, any projections depend on all sorts of
demographic, technological, and macroeconomic factors that are hard to
predict with certainty. For example, what will be our birth and immigra-
tion rates, how long will people live, and how fast will the economy grow?
The Congressional Budget Office (CBO) helps out here by issuing long-
term forecasts that analysts can adopt either wholesale or with specified
adjustments.

The second problem is how to organize our projections of the long-
term fiscal picture into a specific measure. This depends on what we are interested in measuring, which depends on why we care about the long-term
fiscal picture to begin with.

Alternative Measures of the Long-Term Fiscal Picture

Assumptions about Future Policy. In preparing a long-term fiscal measure,
even if one accepts the CBO's economic and demographic projections,
which some regard as unduly optimistic,[1] one must decide what future

policies to assume. For Medicare and Social Security, this simply requires applying the rules on the books for the indefinite future. This is what the Medicare and Social Security Trustees do, although they restrict themselves to a seventy-five-year budget window. This may seem long enough, since few adults expect to be alive in seventy-five years. Yet, if we so restrict the inquiry, then each year the fiscal picture will seem to worsen, even with no surprises and no new information, simply because an extra out-year has entered the computation. The use of an unlimited time horizon avoids this perverse result, and thereby offers a more meaningful long-term picture.[2]

Other areas of policy projection require more nuanced judgment, as well as greater skepticism regarding official CBO forecasts. Consider the government's discretionary spending, which includes everything (such as national defense) that is budgeted annually rather than being fixed in advance like entitlements spending. The CBO assumes that such spending will grow only at the rate of inflation—an assumption tantamount to predicting that discretionary spending will gradually be phased out relative to the economy and population. A more realistic view—particularly in the post-9/11 world, where homeland security issues loom large—would hold that discretionary spending is likely at least to keep pace with population growth and perhaps gross domestic product (GDP).[3]

Policy projection is also difficult under the income tax. While normally one could just project forward the laws on the books, Congress in 2001 and 2003 adopted rules that call for a different approach. It enacted major tax-cut legislation that after only a few years would supposedly lead to the restoration of prior law. These sunsets, however, were merely parliamentary maneuvers to evade the Senate budget rules, which would have required an unattainable sixty votes in favor of the Acts if drafted in accordance with the proponents' intent that they remain in effect indefinitely. No one could seriously maintain that the sunsets represent either current policy or a likely outcome,[4] but the CBO uses them in preparing long-term forecasts.

The Fiscal Gap as a Flow and as a Stock. The next question is what measure to use in describing the long-term fiscal picture. One approach is to estimate the fiscal gap. Auerbach, Gale, and Orszag (2002, 12) define this as "the size of the long-run increase in taxes or reductions in non-interest expenditures (as a constant share of GDP) that would be required immediately" in order to keep current government debt constant as a percentage of GDP. In illustration, suppose that the fiscal gap is 2 percent at a time when GDP is $10 trillion (approximately its 2001 level). This means that taxes would have to increase immediately by 2 percent of GDP, or $200 billion annually, and then keep growing at the same pace as GDP, in order to achieve fiscal stability.[5]

In that formulation, the fiscal gap is stated as a flow, like the annual budget deficit or the amount you must pay each year on a bank loan. The fiscal gap can also be stated as a stock, like the national debt or the principal you owe on a bank loan. To state the fiscal gap as a stock rather than as a flow, one must determine the present value, under an appropriate interest or discount rate, of the annual tax increase amounts that the flow measure implies. Using G to denominate the real growth rate of GDP, and R to denominate the real interest rate, the stock fiscal gap can be stated as the flow fiscal gap divided by $(R - G)$.[6]

In illustration, suppose again that GDP is $10 trillion and that the flow fiscal gap is 2 percent, or $200 billion at the current GDP level. Assume further that R is 3 percent, as in the Medicare Trustees' intermediate forecasts, and that G is 1.5 percent, its average since the end of World War II. Under these assumptions, the stock fiscal gap would be $200 billion/ (.03 − .015), or $13.3 trillion.

In fact, however, the currently projected shortfall is much greater than this. The flow fiscal gap was recently estimated at 7.1 percent of GDP under CBO assumptions, or 11.07 percent if revised to reflect a more reasonable view of the path of discretionary spending and current tax policy (Auerbach, Gale, and Orszag 2002, table 4). This suggests that a tax increase of about $710 billion to $1.107 trillion was needed, at the current GDP level of about $10 trillion, to achieve long-term fiscal balance. Moreover, under the above assumptions about R and G, it suggests a stock fiscal gap of about $47 trillion under the CBO view, or $74 trillion under the revised view. Tax cuts and spending increases (including with respect to Medicare) that President Bush proposed in 2003 may have pushed the latter estimate past $100 trillion. By contrast, the explicit U.S. public debt, as of mid-2002, was barely over $6 trillion.

If $74 trillion is the best current estimate (in early 2003) of the overall fiscal gap, how would this compare to our having an explicit public debt of $74 trillion? The main difference, leaving aside uncertainty, is that the fiscal gap, as merely an implicit debt under an assumed set of policies, can be renounced through policy change without an act of explicit default. This difference is reduced, however, by the fact that some of the possible policy changes, such as reducing Social Security or Medicare benefits, would be viewed by many people, including influential political actors, as almost on a par with defaulting on the explicit national debt.

Relative Size of Different Pieces of the Fiscal Gap. An overall fiscal gap of $74 trillion (rough though this estimate is) sounds considerably larger than the $17.4 trillion fiscal gap for Medicare (from Saving [2002]) that I noted in the previous chapter. The comparison is inapt, however. Saving used a 5.5 percent discount rate for Medicare, in contrast to the 3 percent rate that I used in converting the 11.07 percent flow measure into a stock measure. Saving justifies his use of such a high discount rate by noting the riskiness of future Medicare benefits (supporting the use of a risk premium). While this is a reasonable way of valuing a risk-averse individual's expected benefit, it does not make sense if the question we ask ourselves is what would happen if current policy continued indefinitely.

Nonetheless, converting the flow fiscal gap into a stock fiscal gap by using a discount rate of 5.5 percent is useful as a device for increasing its comparability to Saving's Medicare estimate. The exercise would yield an estimated stock fiscal gap of $27.7 trillion. If we instead scale up the Medicare fiscal gap to keep it at this percentage of a $74 trillion fiscal gap, it would equal $46.5 trillion. Either way, the Medicare portion would be just under 63 percent of the whole.

This estimate offers another rough window on what sort of rate increase would be needed to eliminate the entire fiscal gap through taxes alone. As we saw in chapter 6, just to eliminate the Medicare fiscal gap, the uncapped (Medicare) portion of the payroll tax might have to increase from its present 2.9 percent rate to between 7 and 12.3 percent (Cutler and Sheiner 2000, 306). If the Medicare fiscal gap is about 60 percent of the whole, then eliminating the entire fiscal gap through this tax might require an increase that was about 100/60 (one and two-thirds times) as great. This implies an uncapped payroll tax rate of from 9.7 percent to 19.6 percent—applying on top of the Social Security portion of the payroll tax, the federal income tax, and all state and local government taxes.

Also of interest is the relative magnitude of various other budgetary slices. Saving (2002), with his 5.5 percent discount rate, estimates the Social Security fiscal gap at $12.92 trillion, or about three-quarters of the Medicare gap. As for the 2001 Tax Act, if assumed to be permanent, by one recent estimate it raised the flow fiscal gap by 1.9 percent of GDP (Auerbach, Gale, and Orszag 2002, 16).[7] This translates to a $12.67 trillion increase in the overall fiscal gap at a 3 percent discount rate. Or, using

Saving's 5.5 percent rate for consistency between the pieces, the increased fiscal gap resulting from the 2001 Act ($4.75 trillion) equals 36.7 percent of the Social Security fiscal gap and 27.3 percent of the Medicare fiscal gap. As for the 2003 budget changes, while at this writing it is too early to estimate them, they could easily add tens of trillions of dollars more to the fiscal gap.

Generational Accounting. The leading alternative to the fiscal gap as a framework for presenting the long-term fiscal picture is generational accounting. This methodology involves looking at *who* would pay for restoring long-term fiscal balance under a given set of assumptions. It can thus be used to show redistributive patterns even in the absence of a fiscal gap.

Generational accounting can take a number of different forms. That of greatest interest here involves computing lifetime net tax rates for the members of different age cohorts. One's lifetime net tax rate is determined by dividing lifetime net taxes (taxes paid minus transfers received) by lifetime income, computed in present value terms from birth. Thus, if you had lifetime income of $5 million, paid lifetime gross taxes of $2 million, and received lifetime transfers of $800,000, your lifetime net tax rate would be ($2 million − $800,000)/$5 million, or 24 percent.

If generational accounting computations were made by assuming that current policy will continue indefinitely without regard to the fiscal gap, it would be ignoring the principle that everything must ultimately be paid for. Yet current policy does not tell us how the fiscal gap will be eliminated. Moreover, if one assumed a particular method of eliminating it, one would no longer be making an estimate about current policy (although the exercise might have value as an attempted prediction about actual long-term policy). The solution that generational accounting's proponents have adopted, for purposes of describing current policy, is to treat the entire fiscal gap as being eliminated through a net tax increase on future generations.

The operating assumption, therefore, is that everyone alive today, including newborns, will not have to pay for any of the fiscal gap, leaving those born next year or thereafter to bear it in full. This is concededly unrealistic, and meant to provide "an informative counterfactual, not a likely policy scenario," but it is defended as "deliver[ing] a clear message about the need for policy adjustments" (Kotlikoff 2001, 22). Generational accounting's main punchline, therefore, in terms of the fiscal gap, is provided by comparing the lifetime net tax rate for future generations to that for newborns (since its treatment of the fiscal gap is a key difference between the two). The ratio between the latter and the former has been called a measure of fiscal policy's overall "generational imbalance" (Kotlikoff 2001).

The president's annual budget briefly included generational accounting forecasts, but ceased doing so during the Clinton administration, reportedly because senior officials found them too embarrassing given the political emphasis that was being placed on current budget surpluses. Generational accounting proponents have continued to issue periodic forecasts, using CBO projections but with certain revisions, such as to the present course of tax policy and discretionary spending, and to discount and growth rates. At this writing, the most recent forecast shows lifetime net tax rates of 35.81 percent for future generations and 17.68 percent for current newborns, leading to a generational imbalance measure of 102.52 percent (Kotlikoff 2001, table 1).

A measure of generational imbalance does not have the same immediate implications for sustainability as the stock fiscal gap. For example, a 100 percent increase in lifetime net tax rates, if from 1 percent to 2 percent, might strike us as a matter of near indifference. However, a high projected lifetime net tax rate for future generations indicates that current policy is unsustainable. For example, a 35.81 percent lifetime net tax rate implies a considerably higher gross tax rate, before transfers are taken into account. Thus, the (actual or perceived) marginal tax rate implied by a 35.81 percent net rate is probably above politically or economically feasible levels.

Resilience of the Estimates

Measures of the fiscal gap and generational imbalance can change significantly from year to year in response to new economic data and long-term projections. Thus, the two immediate precursors of the 2002 estimate of an 11.07 percent fiscal gap had placed it at 4.14 percent (Auerbach and Gale 2001) and 1.36 percent (Auerbach and Gale 2000). Under generational accounting, the estimated lifetime net tax rate for future generations had stood in 1991 at 84.4 percent, as compared to the 2001 figure of 35.81 percent.

Even at any moment, long-term projections are enormously sensitive to one's underlying assumptions. For example, in the case of the stock fiscal gap, suppose we raise R (the discount rate) from 3 percent to 4 percent, and cut G (the assumed growth rate for GDP) from 1.5 percent to 1 percent. Even keeping all other assumptions the same, the stock fiscal gap would be cut in half. The estimated more-than-doubling of the fiscal gap between 2000 and 2001 was mainly attributable to a change in CBO assumptions concerning the growth rate for Medicare and Medicaid spending (Auerbach and Gale 2001, 12). It is worth considering, therefore, how the measures' sensitivity to contested and changeable inputs should affect our evaluation of them.

Clearly, we should not operate under the misapprehension that any of the estimates are at all precise. Long-range forecasts unavoidably rest on assumptions that are uncertain, ambiguous, changeable, and controversial. Should we therefore disregard them, or at least discount them for the uncertainty? If you answer this question yes, then presumably you also favor not worrying, say, about the risk of terrorism if its likelihood and magnitude cannot be pinpointed accurately. Mere uncertainty, if accompanied by risk aversion, calls for giving adverse long-term fiscal estimates greater heed, rather than less (Auerbach and Hassett 2001, 91). And even if we can hope that the estimates will gradually improve, it is just as likely that they will grow worse if they make unbiased use of the best available current information.

It is reasonable to ask, however, just how resilient the claim of a long-term fiscal gap is. Might the current picture change just as suddenly as the annual budget picture, which in recent years suddenly switched from deficit to surplus and back again? Unlike the short-term picture, however, the long-term one has consistently retained the same sign. This reflects that its principal cause, population aging due to increasing life expectancy, has been an ongoing process and is expected to continue (Lee and Edwards 2002, 16–18). Thus, even conservative extrapolations suggest that healthcare expenditure on the elderly will continue to rise significantly relative to GDP (Fuchs 1998a, 4).

What about economic growth? History provides various examples of countries, such as England after the Napoleonic Wars and the United States after the Civil War, that simply outgrew explicit public debts that contemporary commentators had feared might prove ruinous (Shaviro 1997, 20–21, 32).

Over the long term, however, the fiscal gap is somewhat growth-proof. Not only taxes but various expenditure programs are pegged to GDP over the long run. Whether or not this is the case for discretionary government spending, for Social Security and Medicare it verges on being explicit. Social Security benefits rise with career earnings and are pegged to productivity growth. Thus, Social Security benefits should tend over time to keep pace with GDP, although they do not fluctuate annually with the business cycle. Over the long term, Medicare expenditures also rise in lockstep with GDP to the extent that the healthcare sector has a constant relative size. If healthcare grows faster than GDP but in correlation with it, growth can actually widen the fiscal gap.

A further concern about the fiscal gap is that it may itself dampen economic growth. If tax hikes are needed to finance Social Security and Medicare benefits over the next few decades, the result may be capital shallowing, or reduced per capita saving and investment (Kotlikoff 2001, 32–35). Accordingly, even insofar as the fiscal gap is not growth-proof, the malady might crowd out the cure.

In sum, therefore, the fiscal gap appears to be highly resilient to possible changes over time. Thus, an economic expansion that made future Americans far wealthier than expected would fail to "help" very much. This should alert us, however, to the fact that something is missing from the analysis thus far. How could it possibly *not* help to grow richer, when the underlying question is what set of commitments we can afford?

An analogy may help to sharpen the issue. Suppose a high-earning corporate executive and his nonworking spouse get divorced. Having incompetent lawyers, they reach the following alimony agreement: Each year he will pay her 30 percent of his salary, and she will get 50 percent of his salary. Thus, if he earns a million dollars next year, he is supposed to pay $300,000, and she is supposed to get $500,000. Just like our fiscal policy, this obviously does not add up. She cannot get from him more than he pays her. Moreover, the financial gap in their agreement is growth-proof, since both sides of the ledger are pegged to his salary. Even if he earns a billion dollars rather than a million, there will still be a 20 percent difference between what he is supposed to pay and what she is supposed to get. Growth in his salary, therefore, does not "help."

Needless to say, however, in truth it really does help. Each of them would be better off losing the dispute over their shares at a salary of $2 million than winning it at a salary of $1 million. So what really is the problem, whether here or in the actual federal budgetary case?

Why Does the Fiscal Gap Matter?

In both the alimony and the federal budgetary cases, one could call the problem merely one of temporary misspecification. That which cannot happen will not happen, and the parties have not yet decided or announced what actually will happen. Yet why is this anything to worry about? Unfeasible policy statements are just words, after all. They do not inherently cause any harm, and will surely in due course be changed.

To see why the fiscal gap is a problem after all, we can start with the alimony case. Suppose the husband, having looked only at the clause concerning his own payments, spends 70 percent of his after-tax salary, while the wife, having looked only at the clause concerning her receipts, uses credit to spend 50 percent. Or suppose they both understand the problem, but cannot plan properly due to uncertainty about its resolution.

Another possibility is that their differing expectations will lead them to go to war in a mutually destructive fashion. Thus, they might incur high legal fees in battling out what the settlement really requires. Or the husband might quit his job and waste his savings, lest his wages or bank account be garnished for back-payments if he loses.

The problems potentially resulting from the fiscal gap are similar, and include the following:

1. *Systematic error.* People who are alive today must make long-term plans that reflect, among other factors, their expectations concerning future government policy. Those who expect the retirement benefits that current policy seems to promise may learn that they have saved too little if the benefits are significantly reduced.

2. *Needless uncertainty.* Even to the extent that today's individuals understand the risk that their retirement benefits will be reduced, the absence of an agreed long-term policy path may hamper their long-term planning. Some people, for example, might end up tightening their belts too much as insurance against the downside of really sizable benefit reduction.

3. *Harmful resolution of the policy misspecification.* Ignoring the fiscal gap until a crisis is at hand may prompt panicky last-minute responses by the political system that could have been avoided by planning further in advance. An example might be printing money, at the risk of hyperinflation, in order to keep things going a bit longer. Or the government might engage in some sort of default or confiscation that needlessly harms people's confidence in its commitments.

4. *Loss of policy options over time.* Since time moves relentlessly forward, not backward, delay in eliminating the fiscal gap continually reduces the available means of eliminating it. In effect, not to decide is gradually to decide, and perhaps with less transparency than if the issues were publicly debated and resolved up front.

With respect to generational distribution, once the members of a given age cohort have died, they can no longer be asked to share in the pain of tax increases or benefit reductions. Even while they are alive, with each year the opportunity to make them share the burden through general income and payroll tax increases (or benefit reductions once they reach retirement) grows less. So does the opportunity to increase their share of the burden without leaving them with too little saving for their own retirements.

To the extent that we make a given age cohort pay more but do so later rather than sooner, we may seriously undermine the forced saving policy that underlies both Medicare and Social Security. People may overspend during their working careers if the extra burden is only imposed later. Moreover, to the extent that delay necessitates cutting people's Medicare benefits rather than raising their income and payroll taxes, we may undermine the Medicare policy of requiring that they allocate some minimum portion of their lifetime resources to retirement healthcare. If the Social Security and Medicare policies are well conceived, therefore, delay may hurt people even insofar as it does not change their lifetime incomes.

Implications of the Fiscal Gap for Medicare

Returning more systematically to the implications for Medicare, we have seen that the overall fiscal gap is really what matters. Yet Medicare is probably responsible for about 60 percent of the whole. This is not a question of blame. Medicare is a program that our legislators enacted to general acclaim, not an individual who was capable of good or bad judgment. The 60 percent figure suggests, however, that Medicare's long-term expenditure commitments under present policy are likely to face enormous pressure in the future unless (and even if) we are willing to countenance huge tax increases to back them up.

Given the need for forced saving and retirement health insurance, as well as the general disadvantages of a large fiscal gap, something should be done, and the sooner the better. The fiscal gap only grows larger (absent favorable shocks) if we defer addressing it. For example, a decade's delay in taking corrective action is estimated to raise the flow fiscal gap to 12.5 percent of GDP (Auerbach, Gale, and Orszag 2002, 15), and thus the stock fiscal gap to $96.7 trillion.[8] Delay also keeps in place for longer the uncertainty and systematic planning errors that may result from a fiscal gap. And it gradually reduces or eliminates options to make current seniors share in the burden of taking corrective action, and to make current workers share without reducing their forced retirement saving.

Summary

The Medicare stock fiscal gap may exceed $45 trillion if we use a discount rate that treats its benefits as certain. This fiscal gap might not matter if projections for the rest of our current tax and spending commitments suggested that we could meet the shortfall without otherwise changing course significantly. In fact, however, the broader picture is considerably worse than that for Medicare alone. The overall fiscal gap, converted from a flow to stock by using reasonable (albeit contestable) assumptions, may be estimated at $74 trillion. By contrast, the explicit national debt (as of mid-2002) is just over $6 trillion.

Despite long-term estimates' volatility, the prediction of a long-term fiscal gap is resilient. The underlying trend of increasing life expectancy is considered stable. Greater-than-expected economic growth might help up to a point, but the fiscal gap is to some extent growth-proof or pegged to GDP over the long term. In addition, volatility suggests that the fiscal gap could grow over time as well as shrink.

Growth-proof though the fiscal gap may be, it surely is better to live in a rich society with a large gap than in a poor society that has announced sustainable long-term policies. Nonetheless, a fiscal gap can do significant harm, such as by causing people to plan poorly or face needless uncertainty. Delay in addressing it also gradually eliminates the opportunity to share burdens with older generations and to maintain needed retirement saving.

The fiscal gap therefore ought to be narrowed sooner rather than later and in a manner that reaches all living age cohorts. And Medicare spending must be rationalized, not just because waste is always worth eliminating, but also to ensure that the inevitable cuts reach as low a proportion of muscle and bone (relative to fat) as possible.

8

Paying for Medicare I: Benefits

MEDICARE inevitably will play a role in narrowing the fiscal gap. Three main instruments (apart from lowering non-Medicare spending) are available. The first, discussed in this chapter, is changing the healthcare benefits that it provides. The other two, discussed in ensuing chapters, are to increase enrollee contributions or various taxes.

Supply-Side Cost Controls

Many experts have been eager to see Medicare join private sector health insurance in making a wholesale shift to managed care. As Henry Aaron, a skeptic about managed care, has noted, even if the approach does not succeed in restraining waste without unduly rationing needed care, "the alternative is not a return to traditional fee-for-service Medicare. The cost of unrestricted moral hazard operating in a field as dynamic as medicine is unsupportable" (Aaron 1999, 60).[1]

Existing Medicare + Choice, while it gives the program a toe in the managed care waters, poses lesser design issues than would a thoroughgoing transformation. Medicare + Choice covers only a subclass of seniors, generally with above-average health, and presumably showing by their participation that they are comfortable with choosing between plans. In addition, it can function without vigorous nationwide competition between participating HMOs, given the fee-for-service fallback. Even so, however, the program has been plagued by HMO withdrawals that in some cases have left subscribers stranded until they could return to fee-for-service Medicare (Cohn 2001), and that would be wholly unacceptable if Medicare HMOs were a larger proportion of the whole. Moreover, the central managed care issue of how to balance cost-saving against quality has been forestalled by the simple expedient of barring price competition and designing Medicare + Choice so that it costs rather than saves the government money.

Converting Medicare wholesale to managed care would not be easy given the intractability of the underlying incentive problems in determining what medical treatment individuals should get. The incentive to demand too much care if you are not paying for it, or too little if you lack foresight and ignore others' altruistic preferences for giving you health-care, cannot be perfectly corrected by any plausible means. Managed care gives providers both tools and a financial incentive to tighten the screws, but it must rely on regulation, standards of medical practice, and the in-centive to compete for satisfied customers in order to supply countervail-ing pressure to offer needed care. The payoff to competition, however, requires not only that competition be vigorous enough in a given market, but also that consumers be sufficiently discerning of quality in order to protect their interests (while not demanding waste) through the exercise of choice. And this, in turn, leads us back to the fundamental incentive prob-lem in healthcare no matter how financed: the agency costs implied by consumers' need to rely on the superior expertise of professionals, such as doctors, who may have their own preferences and interests.

Has private sector managed care for people under age sixty-five found a reasonable balance between cost-saving and preserving quality? There is evidence of failure, at least relative to hopes or expectations, in both di-rections. On the one hand, managed care is increasingly regarded by ex-perts as having largely failed to control rising healthcare costs. In part, this failure reflects the political and legal pressures on HMOs to back off from imposing significant limits. Rationing of healthcare may end up being un-avoidable at some point, and when that day comes private sector managed care organizations may play an important role. At least for now, however, the prevailing political, legal, and market equilibrium does not permit them to impose effective limits.

If HMOs have therefore arguably rationed care too little, there also is a widespread view that they have done it too much. Criticism of HMOs for callously denying needed care has become not only a fruitful political and legal issue, but also a staple of popular culture, as in the recent Hollywood potboiler, *John Q,* that featured a gun-waving vigilante (Denzel Wash-ington, as the "hero") acting like an al Qaeda operative in a crowded emergency room. HMOs' unpopularity proves little, however. Insurance claims adjusters are not popular either, yet presumably we need them to have affordable insurance.[2]

Accordingly, despite the widespread grumbling about managed care, it still may be an improvement over fee-for-service coverage. Certainly, people with money at stake have overwhelmingly cast their dollar votes in its favor as between the two. Yet, even if managed care were doing better than it is, extending it to most or all Medicare enrollees would pose greater challenges than it has faced so far.

A convenient way to convert Medicare into a managed care system would be by offering enrollees vouchers that they could use to select the plan of their choice. For example, vouchers could be set in relation to the cost of the cheapest acceptable plan, and enrollees permitted to top up the coverage by adding their own cash if they liked. This would reverse current Medicare's no-topping-up policy, but in the hope of improving service for everyone. "Vouchers empower individuals by allowing them to choose their service provider" (Reischauer 2000, 416), thus permitting them to tailor their coverage to their needs and inducing providers to compete for their business. So long as voucher recipients are "adequately informed and able decisionmakers . . . [they may be able to] make choices that meet their needs better than would a 'one size fits all' government program" (416–17).

Unfortunately, many seniors, especially if in poor health, are poorly situated to exercise the informed consumer choice that the realization of these advantages requires. Moreover, the enormous variability in seniors' health status might lead to biased selection problems like those that affect Medicare + Choice today, but on a larger scale. In managed care's present realm, such problems, while by no means absent, are less acute. Employers furnish providers with large, diverse pools of enrollees who have in effect been preselected for their general good health and ability to negotiate the economic choices implied by holding a job.

How to address the problems posed by Medicare managed care has been the subject of various prominent proposals[3] and an increasingly voluminous literature,[4] analyzing a host of difficult institutional issues that turn on various parties' incentives, opportunities, and information. Such an analysis lies beyond this book's focus on questions of who pays rather than who chooses. However, even in a best-case scenario where the switch was made promptly and saved money without worsening seniors' healthcare, Medicare would still face a significant fiscal shortfall plus all of the distributional issues that exist today. So shifting to managed care is an important possible option, but only very marginally an alternative to other Medicare changes.

Shifting from a Defined-Benefit to a Defined-Contribution Structure

A shift to managed care would facilitate rethinking Medicare's current character as a defined-benefit (DB) rather than a defined-contribution (DC) plan. Under a DB managed care plan, Medicare might solicit competitive bids that offered a specified set of services, with successful bidders being selected on the basis of both price and quality. Through the use of Medicare vouchers or otherwise, enrollees might be charged for some or all of the price difference if they selected a costlier plan. They would not, however, bear the brunt of general cost increases in providing the defined benefits, since these would be built into the value of the voucher.

By contrast, under a DC managed care plan, Congress might decide how much to spend on buying annual healthcare coverage for enrollees, rather than specifying the required benefit level. Competitive bids might differ in what they offered for the price, although (just as in the DB setting) seniors could be given high-cost and low-cost alternatives. Once again, vouchers might be used, but here their value would be set by Congress rather than emerging from the bidding process. Enrollees would therefore bear the risk of relative price growth in the healthcare sector.

The main issue raised by the choice between DB and DC structures for Medicare is how the risk of relative price growth should be allocated between enrollees and the alternative risk bearers, who presumably are the taxpayers in younger age cohorts. At least, this is the question posed by the DB versus DC choice if Congress is not likely to end up doing the same thing either way, as a consequence of adjusting either the benefits it mandates or the contributions it makes.

If we start by thinking only about the seniors who are enrolled in Medicare at a given time, it seems natural to conclude that the DB structure makes for better social insurance. If technologically feasible care improves, and thus you want to spend more on your own care, it permits you to do so. Or more precisely, this happens if the new treatments fall within existing covered categories. The dramatic growth of prescription drug expenditures in recent decades presents an important counterexample, because here Medicare did not reach the category in which there was growth.

Even where a DB plan does automatically grow with the healthcare sector, however, there is a problem. The counterparties to the seniors' technology "bet," people in younger age cohorts, may be similarly affected by the same trends. Expanding what doctors can do if you are sick presumably increases the marginal value of a dollar to them in the future, as well as to seniors at present. So, even if we want to offer seniors some protection, on the ground that they are at a stage of life where they can no longer save more of their earnings in response to healthcare trends, it does not necessarily follow that we should hand the entire cost to younger generations.

If we would like the ultimate risk-sharing to lie somewhere in between the outcomes that would follow from using unadjusted DB and DC approaches, then the choice should turn on issues of political economy. Which approach is likely to drive Congress closer to adopting an optimal solution? From such a standpoint, the case for preferring a DC structure is quite strong. It would require explicitly budgeted spending increases to adjust for rising relative healthcare costs, requiring seniors to compete in the political arena with rival claimants. Under a DB structure, by contrast, seniors get spending increases automatically. The politics of the last forty years seem to indicate that seniors' political clout is more likely to be too great than too small.

These political economy advantages of the DC approach do not require converting Medicare into a managed-care system. The basic idea would be for Congress to set Medicare's budget (or at least a target expenditure level) on an annual basis, rather than simply specifying the benefits that are allowed. Or, to lessen the departure from Medicare's current legal status as an entitlement, the annual budget could rise automatically with inflation or GDP in the absence of congressional action.

Within Medicare's current structure, this might involve having the available benefits for a given year depend on what Congress set as the expenditure level through its annual budget, with benefits depending on what was affordable given the appropriation. For example, private insurers might make competitive bids to provide fee-for-service coverage in exchange for the per-enrollee compensation that Congress had specified.

Benefit Cuts

Whether or not Medicare shifts to managed care or a DC structure, there is likely to be fiscal pressure for benefit cuts. The leading possibilities (leaving copayments for the next chapter) include the following.

Raising the Medicare Eligibility Age

The 10 percent increase in life expectancies since Medicare was enacted naturally brings to mind the idea of raising the Medicare eligibility age. Social Security is already making such a change, albeit very slowly (Shaviro 2000a, 16), and proposals to do something similar in Medicare have begun to surface (Moon 1996, 196 n. 9).

To evaluate such proposals, it helps to begin by asking how the Medicare retirement age should be set. Suppose we think of Medicare as generally being needed at retirement, because at that point your income declines and you may lose your employer-provided health insurance. If we thought that enrollees' retirement ages were somehow fixed, and thus not subject to being influenced by Medicare, we might pick a standard retirement age within the population as the point when eligibility should start. This, presumably, is how age sixty-five was selected when Medicare was created in 1965 (and Social Security in 1935).

As it happens, retirement age has been relatively constant over the last few decades, rather than increasing alongside life expectancy. This, however, may partly reflect Medicare's influence. By making employer-provided health insurance partly redundant, Medicare has the same incentive effect as taxing those benefits at a steep marginal rate. The value of an employer's compensation package may therefore decline significantly at the point when a worker becomes Medicare eligible. Medicare also may influence social norms regarding when to retire.

Suppose we were to find that people at age seventy today are on average just about as healthy as people were at age sixty-five several decades ago. Then the case for increasing the Medicare eligibility age to seventy—perhaps gradually or after a delay so that people could plan for the new rule—would be extremely compelling. Unfortunately, however, there is evidence that people's health levels in their sixties are not improving commensurately with life expectancy (Poterba and Summers 1986). Many workers still experience significant health problems at this stage that push them toward retirement and complicate the purchase of retirement coverage, because given risks have been resolved unfavorably (Moon 1996, 188). So the case for increasing the Medicare eligibility age is not quite so easy.

From this perspective, it helps to return to some of the basic social insurance issues raised by Medicare's Samuelson financing (discussed in chapter 6). If demographic trends create an expectation that the members of a given age cohort will be retired for longer, they are likely to need more retirement saving. If intergenerational transfers cannot change, then the sole mechanism for accomplishing this is for people to save more during their working years. To the extent that they do not respond adequately on a voluntary basis, this requires increasing their taxes without commensurately increasing government spending on their consumption.

Once we put intergenerational transfers back on the table, the fact that a given age cohort is long-lived might induce us to want to make greater transfers to it, which indeed is the consequence of Samuelson financing. But this does not imply handing the entire bill to members of future generations, whose life expectancies will be greater still.

We therefore may want to ensure that current seniors' Medicare benefits (net of taxes) increase by less than the amount implied by Samuelson financing. Raising the eligibility age would accomplish this, but not in a very good way if the retirement age is relatively fixed. After all, if you were rationally allocating a fixed budget on your retirement coverage, you presumably would spread it in some fashion over the entire retirement period, rather than entirely eliminating a couple of years' coverage.

Accordingly, the argument for raising the Medicare eligibility age, in preference to alternative benefit cuts, rests on the possibility that this would influence retirement decisions. Working longer makes sense, even if your health is less than perfect, if your expected retirement needs have increased. So we might want to raise the Medicare eligibility age as a way of inducing people to work longer, so that they will accumulate more resources in response to their greater retirement needs.

Reducing Coverage of Near-Death Expenditure

Another possible source of Medicare benefit cuts pertains to healthcare expenditures near the end of life. According to a recent study, 24 percent of Medicare's healthcare expenditures are for people who die within a year of receiving the care, and 18 percent are for people who die within six months (Garber, MaCurdy, and McClellan 1998, 253). To the extent that this represents futile care—for example, aggressive surgery to aid cancer patients who have no significant chance of being helped by it—reducing it would save money while not harming (and perhaps even helping) the people whose care was reduced.

Unfortunately, however, it is hard to tell in advance what care is futile and which patients are going to die. The most common causes of death among the elderly are chronic diseases that create a need for ongoing care without indicating that death is certain to be imminent (264). Thus, significant cost-saving may not be possible here without risking the denial of care that might have done much good.

Over time, our society may increasingly face healthcare rationing issues that involve this risk. Medicare is unlikely to be ahead of the curve in addressing it, however.

Reducing Payment Rates to Medicare Providers

Among voter focus groups, if not in the interest-group-infested waters of Capitol Hill, there is probably no more appealing Medicare change than slashing payments to healthcare providers. Doctors, hospitals, drug companies, and HMOs are all convenient whipping boys for rising Medicare costs. To some extent, moreover, this status is deserved, albeit more as a matter of flawed incentives than of a *Mr. Smith Goes to Washington–*

style morality play. Given the barriers to informed oversight by patients and to market-sensitive pricing by centralized administrative fiat, providers have significant opportunities to make money, not only through demand inducement but by gaming Medicare's Proposed Payment System (PPS).

Up to a point, therefore, Medicare may be able to reduce costs by rationalizing PPS or replacing it with a fundamentally different approach. The latter alternative might involve making greater use of competitive bidding (Antos 1998, 49), rather than using thousands of centrally administered prices. Even within PPS, there may be room to address such common practices as inflating diagnoses so they will qualify for higher reimbursement, or unbundling services so that they can be billed separately. Doing so is impeded, however, not just by administrative and information problems but by healthcare providers' political clout in Congress.

If allowed by Congress to cut costs aggressively, the Center for Medicare and Medicaid Services could wield the considerable market power that Medicare possesses by virtue of its having in effect organized seniors as a cartel. We should keep in mind, however, that such exercises of consumer-side monopsony power, as of producer-side monopoly power, may lead to inefficiency and undersupply. In addition, aggressive Medicare price-cutting may function as an ostensibly one-time taking from people and firms with large sunk costs in the healthcare industry, and thus who cannot readily respond by shifting to some other business. The problem with such ostensibly one-time takings (as discussed more generally in Shaviro 2000b) is that they may send an adverse signal to those who are considering similar (or perhaps any) sunk-cost investment in the future, thereby over time potentially discouraging medical or other investment.

So reducing payments to Medicare providers may have merit up to a point, but is also prone to political misuse. Perhaps we should be comforted that bad political incentives lurk on both sides of the issue, pitting demagogy and the lure of easy money against significant interest group power. It is hard to be confident, however, that the balance between the two will come out right.

Reducing Medicare Expenditure in High-Cost Areas

Medicare's redistribution from regions where healthcare is relatively cheap, such as Minneapolis, to those where, for the same medical condition, it is relatively costly, such as Miami, is probably undesirable. The issue is mainly one of efficiency, given the evidence that more intensive treatment in high-cost areas results neither in better healthcare outcomes nor in greater consumer satisfaction. Medicare not only subsidizes the relatively wasteful treatment norms in high-cost areas, but reduces the incentive to consider relative healthcare costs in deciding where to live. Even without a fiscal gap, therefore, we might want to reduce Medicare expenditure in high-cost areas.

If Medicare were revised to use vouchers in subsidizing enrollees' purchase of health insurance, regional disparities in treatment cost for a given condition could easily be addressed by making the vouchers nationally uniform, or at least not fully adjusted for regional cost differences. Within the current system, however, reform is more difficult. Regional cost variations result, after all, not from any use of regionalized fee schedules, but from differences in standard medical practice. The possibilities that have been suggested include imposing volume-performance standards on particular medical staffs, and (as has been done in Canada) limiting reimbursements to overserved areas (Skinner and Fisher 1997, 422–23).

Benefit Expansion

Despite the long-term fiscal picture, benefit expansion is (unsurprisingly) more widely discussed than benefit contraction. In particular, adding prescription drug coverage has recently become a prominent political issue, reflecting technological developments that have greatly increased the costs that seniors incur (and the medical benefit they can derive) from using prescription drugs. Congress in 2003 seemed poised to add some such coverage, unless political disputes regarding exactly how to do it led (once again) to stalemate. Catastrophic and long-term care, while less politically salient (especially given the 1988 legislative fiasco), have a strong following among experts who recognize their insurance value.

In evaluating such changes, it is useful to separate two distinct questions. The first is how Medicare should allocate its costs between alternative benefits. The second is how rich the coverage should be overall.

From the standpoint of allocating total Medicare costs that are hypothetically fixed, it seems clear that prescription drug and catastrophic coverage should be provided. They make up a significant component of seniors' medical risk. Medicare's failure to add them promptly has reflected political rigidities that one would not expect to find under conditions of market competition.

With regard to a prescription drug benefit, however, we should keep in mind that, by a recent measure, two-thirds of Medicare enrollees already have coverage of some kind through their supplemental insurance (McClellan 2000b, 35)—although rising prescription drug costs may be causing this to decline. For enrollees who are already covered, the lure of pre-scription drug coverage through Medicare may have little to do with in-surance. Rather, it may be that, to the extent they no longer have to pay a market price for the benefit, they are getting an extra transfer from younger-age cohorts.

A further concern about Medicare prescription drug coverage is that the constant political temptation to provide first-dollar rather than true insurance coverage (37) may influence the design. Even for seniors who do not currently have the coverage, this would make it merely a transfer with-out risk-spreading benefits, to the extent that it covered expenditures they would have made in any event.

This leads us to the second question, which is how rich overall Medicare coverage should be, given the value of the benefits that enrollees do not presently get. In the abstract, it certainly is true that the amount that we should want to spend on seniors' healthcare is greater if costly pre-scription drugs can now help them. This is an application of the point from earlier chapters that one ought to insure against the "risk" of costly yet valuable treatment options emerging.

Given, however, the political difficulty of restraining transfers to se-niors, there is much to be said for making enrollees pay for any new bene-fits, whether through offsetting benefit cuts or other new taxes and fees. Prescription drug coverage, for example, might help provide the sweet-ener to permit the passage of needed reforms by bundling them together, however arbitrarily.

The Bush administration, in early 2003, was urging exactly this ap-proach by proposing that prescription drug coverage be limited to seniors who chose managed care. However, the difficulty of rationalizing denial of the coverage to seniors in traditional fee-for-service Medicare seemed to be making this a hard sell politically. Combining the benefit with fee and tax increases might have been easier to defend logically.

Summary

The main possibilities for improving (and helping to sustain) Medicare on the benefit side include the following.

    1. *Stronger supply-side cost controls, such as those recently attempted in the private sector through managed care.* This is probably inevitable at some point, in Medicare as well as the private sector, and whether im-posed by market forces or government mandate. Cost-saving through the use of managed care has thus far proven elusive in the private sector, al-though this partly reflects political and legal obstacles that may at some

point be eased. However, cost-saving through the use of managed care might be harder still for Medicare than the private sector to accomplish properly.

2. *Shifting from a defined-benefit (DB) to a defined-contribution (DC) structure.* Medicare's current DB structure superficially seems appealing because it enables seniors to take advantage of costly new treatment options (unless, like prescription drugs, they fall outside the covered categories). However, a DB structure lessens workers' incentive to save more for their own retirements by reason of healthcare trends, and shifts the cost to future generations that might have still better (and costlier) treatment options. While shifting to a DC structure might in principle go too far in the other direction, giving seniors no upside if treatment improves, it has political economy advantages, since it prevents the benefit increases from taking effect automatically.

3. *Reductions in Medicare benefits.* Raising the Medicare eligibility age is desirable if effective in inducing later retirement, but probably not otherwise. Reducing near-death health expenditure would be desirable if one could identify treatment with little or no expected benefit, but that is hard to do. Cutting payments to Medicare providers may make sense given defects in Medicare's centrally administered cost structure. However, it risks inducing providers to drop out of Medicare and reduce their investment of human and financial capital in healthcare. Regional variations in the cost of providing healthcare might be addressed by reining in Medicare expenditure in high-cost areas. This could be done through the use of Medicare vouchers that were not fully regionally adjusted or through more conventional regulatory controls.

4. *Benefit expansion.* New benefits for prescription drug coverage, catastrophic care, and long-term care have considerable merit on a net-expenditure-neutral basis. Adding new benefits without funding, however, increases the already-huge fiscal gap. And even fully financing the benefits through payroll and income tax increases would add to the already-huge transfers through the fiscal system from younger to older generations. Any move to adopt new benefits should therefore be packaged politically with other, less popular measures addressing Medicare's design and the fiscal gap.

Paying for Medicare II: Enrollee Contributions

INCREASED enrollee contributions ought to be a part of paying for Medicare for two reasons. First, greater cost consciousness at the margin, in particular for routine healthcare expenditures, is needed to address waste and make Medicare more of a true insurance program. Second, current seniors ought to share with younger generations the burden of narrowing the fiscal gap. Seniors who have retired, however, face only limited income tax liability and no payroll tax liability. They therefore can only be made to pay a significant share through increased enrollee contributions (or the introduction of a consumption tax such as the value-added tax [VAT], which I discuss in chapter 10).

In restructuring Medicare to feature increased enrollee contributions, issues of optimal health insurance design are important but not the entire story. Seniors' broader ability to pay must also be considered. Moreover, we should keep in mind that increasing enrollee contributions results in reducing forced saving through Medicare. Making this all the more significant is the fact that seniors' out-of-pocket healthcare expenditures, which can be quite substantial (Fuchs 1998b, 7), are increasing as well.

Misuse of Medigap to Eliminate Cost-Sharing

An obvious initial change—low-lying fruit in policy terms, whether or not politically—would be to address the misuse of Medigap to wipe out the incentive effects of Medicare copayments. This is no trivial matter. In the famous words attributed to Everett Dirksen, the 1960s Republican Senate leader: "A billion here and a billion there, and pretty soon you're talking real money." Even Dirksen might have been impressed by the estimated $17 to $30 billion annual budgetary cost to Medicare of permitting seniors use private Medigap insurance to cover their Medicare copayments, and thereby to eliminate their cost consciousness at the margin. The point, however, is not just to reduce Medicare spending—which we could drive to zero by eliminating the program—but to target spending that is worth less to the enrollees than the copayments.

In one sense, eliminating this flaw in Medicare would be free money. It would correct what Robert Ball (1998, 37), who as a Johnson administration official helped design the system, has called "a major mistake we made. . . . We had no idea that the Medicare cost-sharing provisions—the copayments and the deductible—would be canceled out by the growth of a medigap industry. . . . The result is that neither the patient nor the physician has an incentive to think twice about the cost of a procedure." From a policy standpoint, the change verges on being a technical correction, avoiding an undesirable result that also happens to provide significant one-shot fiscal relief.

Distributionally and from a practical political standpoint, however, the change would be anything but free money. Seniors who currently use Medigap would feel the effect, and no doubt some would communicate with their congressional representatives about it. To be sure, they would not as a group lose out-of-pocket. Medigap insurers must charge premiums that on average are sufficient to cover the Medicare copayments that they agree to bear. Seniors therefore would lose only insofar as they were less fully insured (the very reason for the change) and now had to use fewer healthcare services that, while evidently not worth the copayments to them, were worth more than zero.

If the Medigap problem is addressed, barring private insurance coverage of low-end copayments is only one possibility. A second is to tax Medigap policyholders (or the companies on a per-policy basis, which amounts to the same thing) for the cost externality that the coverage imposes on Medicare. Some estimates suggest that a tax of about 100 percent on Medigap premiums would be in approximately the correct range (Frech 1999, 115–16). If the price can be set accurately enough, this is preferable to prohibiting Medigap coverage of copayments, because it still permits enrollees to eliminate the variability of these costs at an actuarially fair price.

Reducing Low-End Coverage of Relatively Routine Medical Expenses

Even without the burden of Medigap cross-subsidization, Medicare would be flawed as health insurance by its excessive coverage of routine expenditures. Consider that, in 2003, the Part A deductible for up to sixty days of hospitalization was only $840, while in Part B only a $100 deductible had to be satisfied before the system started offering (in most categories) 80 percent coverage.

The potential to reduce both waste and Medicare outlays through increased cost-sharing is therefore quite substantial. For example, as of several years ago, an annual deductible of $1,500 for Parts A and B combined would have resulted in estimated annual budgetary savings of $9 billion

(Moon 1996, 182)—surely high enough to meet the Everett Dirksen "real money" standard, though not to approach eliminating the fiscal gap. Larger deductibles might also be considered, and might be designed to apply on a lifetime rather than an annual basis. Such proposals would not involve unmanageable administrative difficulty. The problem is mainly political, reflecting "free" healthcare's allure both to the pocketbooks of seniors and to voters who are accustomed to tax-induced overinsurance in the private sector.

If Medicare copayments are ultimately addressed, consideration should be given to "trading in" the deductible for a lower copayment rate across a broader range of expenditures. To illustrate the trade-in, suppose we were considering a $2,500 deductible, followed (for descriptive convenience) by 100 percent reimbursement of medical expenditures. A deductible is simply a copayment where the patient's share is 100 percent. A 50 percent copayment for the first $5,000 of medical expenditures would have exactly the same impact as a $2,500 deductible on enrollees who spent at least $5,000. However, the $5,000/50 percent system would be less generous for those who spent less than $5,000. If one therefore gradually increased the 50 percent copayment range past $5,000, at some point it would match the budgetary effect of the deductible.

One way of choosing between these budgetarily identical alternatives is to ask which provides greater efficiency gains via the increased cost consciousness. A study by Martin Feldstein and Jonathan Gruber (1995) suggests that deductibles generally do less to reduce inefficient overconsumption of medical services than lesser copayments that apply across a broader range. These differences reflect that "the initial increases in cost-sharing have the greatest marginal reduction in deadweight loss, so spreading a moderate cost-sharing increase over a greater sensitive range is more efficient" (Gruber 1998, 48).

Requiring seniors to pay more of their routine healthcare expenses would, of course, change Medicare's distributional policy. From a purely intergenerational standpoint, this might make sense, politics aside, given the argument for transferring more resources to future generations that we expect to have greater consumption opportunities. In principle, however, the efficiency gain could be decoupled from the budgetary and distributional change. If seniors needed to be placated politically, they could be partially compensated for the rise in cost-sharing liability via increased cash grants (for example, through Social Security) that they could spend as they liked. Better a reduced budgetary gain (and accompanying efficiency gain) than none at all.

Even if there is no political need to compensate seniors, increasing their copayments could be problematical for the less well-off. Seniors who are poor enough to qualify for Medicaid presumably could use it as under present law, but some of those who do not quite meet the Medicaid eligibility standards might merit concern as well. This is among the reasons for means-testing Medicare copayments, as I further discuss below.

Higher Medicare Premiums

Increased deductibles or copayments provide only one means of raising seniors' share of the cost of their own healthcare. A second, and possibly complementary, alternative is to increase the premiums they are charged for enrolling in Medicare.

At present, seniors pay nothing to enroll in Part A of Medicare, and $704.40 annually (as of 2003) to enroll in Part B if they do not qualify to have Medicaid pay this amount. The Part B premium, which is pegged at roughly 25 percent of Part B's annual cost, raised $22.3 billion in 2001, or about 9 percent of overall Medicare expenditure. One therefore could have raised another $22 billion by doubling the premium.

A move to double the Part B premiums could easily be rationalized as consistent with Medicare's history. The premiums originally covered 50 percent of Part B's costs, and the change therefore could be described as merely returning Medicare to its roots. A premium increase could also be associated with integrating Parts A and B of Medicare.

However, a more meaningful evaluation of raising Part B premiums would consider the incentive and distributional effects. On the efficiency front, the big difference between raising premiums and raising copayments is that premiums do not affect seniors' cost consciousness at the margin in seeking healthcare. A premium increase, therefore, does not offer commensurate efficiency gain. On the other hand, increasing Medicare premiums may be more appealing on efficiency grounds than using income and payroll tax financing, although this depends on the incentive effects of using Medicaid to help the poorer enrollees. A higher premium for a program that you are certain to enroll in anyway (whether because it still offers good value for money or because participation is mandatory) operates like a lump-sum tax, the Medicaid aspect aside. By contrast, income taxes discourage work and saving, and payroll taxes discourage work.

Distributionally, however, the use of higher premiums instead of income and payroll taxes has the vice of its virtue. As a uniform head tax on enrollees (again, Medicaid aside), it demands the same monetary contribution from a senior just over the Medicaid eligibility line as it does from people on the level of a Warren Buffett or Bill Gates, notwithstanding large differences in ability to pay.

For this reason, some commentators have proposed charging means-related Medicare premiums and/or copayments. This exchanges the virtues and vices of a uniform head tax for those of income or payroll tax financing by responding to differences in ability to pay but creating disincentives to work and save. Such a trade-off is often considered acceptable, as shown by the fiscal system's far greater use of income and payroll taxes than uniform head taxes. In some respects, however, means-testing within Medicare is different from the use of income and payroll tax financing. It also is considerably more controversial, as I discuss next.

Means-Testing for Medicare Copayments and Premiums

Political Economy Significance of Means-Testing

Medicare has never used means-testing for its premiums or copayments. Thus, there might be a perception of fundamental change if either of these enrollee contributions were made to vary with some measure of enrollees' means, such as their current-year income or assets.

It should be clear that this is just a perceptual problem, not one going to the fundamental character of the system. After all, Medicare premiums and copayments are already effectively means-tested insofar as Medicaid may help pay them. We merely have chosen not to define these Medicaid contributions as officially part of Medicare. In addition, Medicare's income and payroll tax financing (which might be considered prepaid mandatory premiums) are income-related. So we are simply playing games if we pretend that means-related premiums or copayments would really involve a fundamental shift of any kind. Still, the fact that means-testing for premiums and copayments might be perceived as a radical departure has potential political significance, whether for good or ill, that needs consideration.

The principal political economy argument against means-testing Medicare premiums and copayments is that it "would likely undermine the strong support that has traditionally gone to Medicare precisely because it is a universal program" rather than one resembling welfare (Moon 1996, 192). Medicare's original drafters "knew the political value of a program that would be viewed as a 'middle-class' entitlement" (193).

The argument appears to be that individuals who reach retirement with limited resources would end up doing worse if we means-tested Medicare premiums and copayments, even though we were trying to favor them relative to well-off retirees. In a lifetime sense, it is hard to believe that they would do worse, even if Medicare benefits were allowed to decline once the perception of universality had been weakened. After all, the program has little if any progressivity as it stands, and Medicare utilization is income-correlated.

So the claim must be that means-testing, by endangering Medicare's political support, would leave poorer seniors worse-off at retirement, even if not in a lifetime sense, by reducing their forced saving and retirement healthcare coverage via the program. Here again, however, the claim is hard to credit. Medicaid and the ability to get emergency room treatment already provide something of a social safety net for senior healthcare. And Medicare benefits would remain universally available to seniors under means-testing, even though the terms of participation would be income-related. Under these conditions, how much should we worry about the risk of reducing slightly the generosity of a program that high-income individuals use more intensively?

More generally, the adage that only middle-class entitlements can adequately protect the interests of the poor is ripe for reexamination. It is true enough that welfare-like benefits may be politically vulnerable if middle-class voters do not regard them with sympathy (although Medicaid has kept going for all these years). Yet the effort to protect aid to the poor by stapling it to middle-class entitlements, the redistributive content of which is deliberately kept obscure, has pitfalls of its own. Rather than accomplishing greater aid to the poor than would otherwise have been politically feasible, it may instead lead to programs that (like Medicare) are not on balance progressive at all, and yet that compete aggressively in the federal budget against programs that would be directed at the poor. In short, try to aid the poor under the guise of a middle-class entitlement, and you may end up doing exactly what you were pretending to do, rather than what you ostensibly wanted to do.

From this perspective, the possibility that Medicare means-testing would weaken political support for the program is conceivably more of a virtue than a vice. In view of seniors' political muscle (exemplified by the American Association of Retired Persons [AARP]), political support for Medicare today is arguably too strong rather than too weak. Medicare already tends to crowd out—and may do so increasingly as demographic factors cause it to grow—a wide range of competing budgetary priorities that cannot draw on comparable political muscle. Not just aid to the poor, but also to children and to future generations might have better prospects if Medicare's aura of universality were weakened. Moreover, desirable Medicare reforms, such as rationalizing benefits, might be easier to accomplish if Medicare were less politically inviolable.

A final political economy point in favor of Medicare means-testing concerns the possibility that, at present, its progressivity is greatly overestimated because people underappreciate the extent to which its benefits are income-correlated. In principle, you can add progressivity anywhere in the fiscal system, and the amount we end up with may reflect the inexorable political balance of power between competing interests. Yet, if an important piece of the system is widely misunderstood, the political equilibrium may be affected. Incorporating means-testing to Medicare, on the stated rationale that it responds to income-correlated Medicare usage, might result in greater (and more accurately understood) progressivity by conforming the reality with the perception.

In sum, while any discussion of political economy effects is inevitably speculative, the impact of means-testing for Medicare premiums and co-payments should be predominantly favorable. It therefore ought to be a part of meeting the fiscal gap, unless its incentive and distributional effects are inferior to those of income and payroll taxation, its closest substitutes.

Means-Testing Compared with Income and Payroll Taxation

From an economic standpoint, the chief concern about means-testing that has been expressed in the literature is that it would discourage work and saving. In the context of analyzing Social Security means-testing, theoretical models (Feldstein 1987) and empirical studies (Neumark and Powers 1999) suggest that work and saving would indeed be adversely affected. Yet this is hardly a surprise insofar as means-testing, if based on income or assets, is equivalent to an income or wealth tax. Suppose that a Medicare means test required enrollees to add one dollar to their Part B Medicare premiums for each $100 by which their net worth exceeded a specified threshold. For enrollees who still subscribed to Part B, this would be identical to levying a 1 percent tax on their net worth above the threshold, without any stated relationship to Medicare. Calling it an increase in the Part B premium does nothing to alter its incentive effects.

Means-testing for Medicare copayments is slightly more complicated, but not fundamentally different. If enrollees' Medicare expenditures were fixed and uniform, the means test would be equivalent to a stand-alone means tax on enrollees. Of course, Medicare expenditures are not fixed, and thus a means test would affect incentives to seek healthcare, as well as to work and save. Moreover, since expenditures are not uniform, the burden imposed by the means test would vary with health condition (and propensity to seek care) even among people with the same means. Yet a means test does not become any less a means tax merely because it happens to be intermingled with a rule requiring increased copayments.[1]

Accordingly, there is every reason to expect an income or asset-based means test to affect work and saving. This, however, is a humdrum "dog bites man" story, not a case of "man bites dog." As a practical matter, deterrence of work and saving comes with the territory of seeking to distribute burdens in relationship to ability to pay (although in the case of a payroll tax, only work incentives are affected). Moreover, given the likely role of income and payroll taxation in narrowing the fiscal gap, avoiding means-testing while one's overall distributional goals remained the same would simply change the instrument that was being used to exert the deterrent effect.

A question of greater interest than whether means-testing would deter work and saving is how it would differ from using income, wealth, or payroll taxes. To avoid conflating this choice with that which lies between the various tax bases, this is best done by comparing a given tax to a means test that uses the same base. Thus, an income tax should be compared to an income-conditioned means test, or a payroll tax to a means test based on career earnings.

Since income-conditioned means tests have been the most discussed, we can start by comparing them to income taxation. Suppose that Medicare premiums and copayments were being increased in any event, but that Congress had to decide whether they should be income-conditioned or uniform, under the stipulation that, in the latter case, comparable overall income redistribution would be held constant via the income tax and welfare systems. How would these alternatives differ from each other?

The use of income-conditioned Medicare premiums and copayments would be distinctive in four main respects. First, it would permit the transitional hit on current seniors to be apportioned based on a measure of ability to pay. Poorer seniors would lose less than richer seniors on a lifetime basis (even though seniors are past their main years of income tax liability), and also would experience a lesser reduction in their forced saving via Medicare. This clearly is an important advantage if current seniors must contribute significantly to narrowing the fiscal gap.

Second, income-conditioning would tend to increase seniors' effective marginal tax rates, taking account of the entire fiscal system, relative to those of younger individuals who were not yet enrolled in Medicare. From the standpoint of efficiency, this is a disadvantage of income-conditioning, since seniors' work decisions are generally more tax responsive than those of people in their prime working years. Leaving the workforce is generally a more realistic alternative for seniors than for younger people (apart from secondary earners among couples).

Third, Medicare' subsidies for health insurance coverage and healthcare expenditure would be more targeted on poorer seniors if premiums and copayments were income-conditioned than if they were uniform. This, however, would improve the efficiency of Medicare's subsidy, which aims to establish a floor on seniors' insurance coverage and receipt of healthcare when needed, rather than to increase their consumption of these items across the board. Wealthier seniors can afford to, and generally do, buy more health insurance coverage and pay more out of their pockets for healthcare than poorer seniors, suggesting that Medicare's subsidies are to a greater extent wasted on them (Pauly 1999c, 70–72).

Finally, income-conditioning Medicare premiums and copayments would make the overall marginal tax rates that seniors faced less transparent. While not without possible political advantages, this suggests a significant danger in the use of means-testing. When the fiscal system uses benefit phase-outs along with explicit taxes without explicitly integrating the two, the lack of coordination may cause policymakers unknowingly to adopt effective marginal tax rates that are clearly too high, in the sense of excessively discouraging work and saving to be worth the distributional benefit. This has resulted, for example, from existing means-testing for such transfers to the poor as Temporary Aid to Needy Families, Food Stamps, the earned income tax credit, and Medicaid. In illustration, as I have elsewhere shown, it is possible for a single parent with two children to be better off earning $10,000 per year than $25,000, once we take account of all income-related taxes and benefit phaseouts (Shaviro 1999, 1196).[2] This is not an inevitable consequence of means-testing, however; it is merely a danger to take into account.

In sum, means-testing of Medicare premiums and copayments probably ought to be adopted. In particular, it has political economy advantages, permits a more equitable burden allocation among current seniors, and better targets Medicare's forced saving and healthcare subsidy. Adopting it does, however, risk creating invisible marginal tax rates on seniors that are simply too high, especially given seniors' tax responsiveness. Means-testing ought to be done with care, therefore, and with an eye to minimizing the incentive to retire relative to the revenues being raised.

Implementing Means-Testing

Even if Medicare means-testing is a good idea in principle, its merits in practice depend on the specific details of its implementation. The relevant design issues, as for taxes generally, pertain to the means test's base, its marginal rates, and the taxpaying unit (such as an individual or household) to which it applies.

Choice of Base I: The Measure of Enrollee Means. The tax base for a Medicare means test is a function of both its intermingled features: the measure of enrollee means that it adopts, and the Medicare features that it affects. The question of how to measure means or material well-being is hardly a novel one. For straightforward or stand-alone taxes that are means-based, enough has been written over the years to fill many libraries. The question of how to define and measure means is broached, at least implicitly, whenever one writes about tax policy, tax reform, or the existing income tax.

In measuring the well-being of seniors who are enrolled in Medicare, two polar alternatives help to define the range of possibilities. The first is lifetime earnings, typically used by economists to measures taxes' and transfers' distributional effects on a lifetime basis. The second is current wealth or net assets. These two measures possess very different virtues. Lifetime earnings focuses on an individual's material well-being throughout life. It avoids treating a high-saver who earned $50,000 a year as more fortunate than a low-saver who earned $1 million a year but spent it all on luxurious living. In effect, it prevents the child who wolfed down his ice cream from demanding half of the slow eater's remaining treat as well. And if we believed that people generally make rational spending choices in keeping with the lifecycle model, differences in retirement saving as between two people with the same lifetime earnings might be thought merely to indicate different preferences.

Wealth, by contrast, possesses the virtues of a snapshot measure. It is more informative about one's ability to pay, for healthcare or anything else, at the moment of measurement. In effect, it recognizes the need of the child who failed to save enough of his food and now is desperately hungry. It thereby responds to our awareness that people often fail to save rationally as dictated by the lifecycle model, and thus that differences in same-earners' retirement saving may reflect differences in planning ability rather than in preference. Yet it does so by rewarding the low-savers for their error, and thus encouraging people to err.

In conventional tax policy terms, the choice between these two measures of seniors' means is closely related to that between income and consumption taxation. On a lifetime basis, a tax on earnings is economically equivalent to a consumption tax if earnings are defined broadly enough.[3] An income tax effectively includes a wealth tax. Henry Simons (1938, 50) famously defined income as the sum of the taxpayer's consumption and change in net worth during the taxable year, and taxing net worth changes (other than those that result from consumption expenditure) is a lot like taxing the net worth itself.[4] So one's general tax policy views might influence one's assessment of lifetime earnings versus wealth as alternative bases for the means test.

A lifetime earnings base would be easy to administer, so long as it used the relatively narrow payroll tax definition of earnings.[5] It would probably be unacceptable, however, given the problem of the one-time high-earner who has nothing left when he retires. The skepticism about people's planning ability that underlies Medicare and Social Security forced saving suggests taking this concern seriously, and thus that lifetime earnings is indeed the wrong base in this setting, even if one generally prefers consumption to income taxation.

A wealth test would pose significant administrative burdens, unless an unduly narrow measure was being used. Under Medicaid, eligibility generally depends on having less than $2,000 in "resources," which generally are cash plus other property that the owner can liquidate or convert into cash (such as savings accounts, certificates of deposit, real property, cars, stocks, and life insurance policies). Items such as homes, household goods, personal effects, and jewelry are excluded. Both the exclusions and the single-threshold character of the Medicaid resources test help to ease its application administratively, but at a high price. The exclusions make it inaccurate as a wealth measure, while the threshold combines severe saving disincentives for people who are just below it with excessively disparate treatment of people just above and below.

Even if such an approach is justified as to Medicaid, where a threshold is unavoidable if one is either eligible or not, it ought not to be used in Medicare means-testing. Thus, in light of the administrative difficulty of attempting to measure all enrollees' wealth so that their contributions can increase only gradually, a wealth test ought to be avoided altogether. A better means to a similar end would be to piggyback on the income measure that already is in use for purposes of the income tax. For seniors who have enough income to be required to file returns, this would involve little in the way of new compliance or administrative burdens. The main problem with it is political, since the means test would then look too much like a tax. As Marilyn Moon (1996, 163) notes, "the income tax is already an unpopular mechanism in general and also bears the baggage of the failure of the MCCA" (the Medicare Catastrophic Coverage Act of 1988).

Use of the income tax would, of course, involve adopting a measure that is highly imperfect as a consequence of Congress's predilection to play games with the tax base (along with the administrative difficulty of trying to measure income accurately). Yet adjustments for purposes of the means test would create compliance and administrative burden, while also posing the question of why Congress should be expected to do any better here than under the income tax itself.

For the most part, therefore, the income tax measure of income should be accepted without modification despite its flaws. However, in light of seniors' significant tax responsiveness when they are considering whether to retire, an earned income exclusion for purposes of the Medicare means test, up to some maximum dollar amount, is probably desirable. The resulting administrative burden would be limited, since federal income tax returns already have a separate line for wages and salary (which, for workers whom the tax law classifies as employees, must be reported by employers on W-2s).

Choice of Base II: Medicare Features That Are Subject to Means-Testing. The Medicare Part B premium, which in 2003 stood at $704.40 per year, is the most commonly mentioned candidate for Medicare means-testing. An income-conditioned increase in the premium would be easy to administer through the income tax if the political obstacles could be overcome. The increase would be equivalent to simply raising seniors' income tax rates, since no incentives would be affected (other than to earn taxable income) for those who still enrolled in Part B.

Income-related copayments would be administratively burdensome, in addition to raising confidentiality issues regarding seniors' financial status, if healthcare providers or insurers were expected to collect them. If Congress were willing to risk the appearance of a tax, however, they could be collected on the income tax return itself. All this would require administratively is an income tax reporting mechanism for determining the benefits that were subject to the extra copayment.[6]

One way of making copayments effectively income-related would be to treat Medicare benefits as themselves taxable income (Moon 1996, 163). This would effectively integrate the Medicare means test with the income tax, thereby helping to avoid the inadvertent creation of excessive marginal tax rates for seniors. Only the income tax rate would apply to an extra dollar that an enrollee earned, rather than the income tax rate plus an increase in copayments that Congress might fail to coordinate properly with the income tax.

To ease the burden on seniors who had little income other than the receipt of Medicare benefits, the percentage of benefits that were includable could start low and rise with other taxable income (excluding earned income up to a ceiling, to limit the disincentive to continue working). This would, however, add complexity and partly undo the marginal tax rate coordination. In view of the insurance arguments for greater high-end than routine coverage, the amount of Medicare benefits that were subject to income tax inclusion could be capped at some dollar amount.

Another approach to the insurance design problem would be to apply income-conditioning to Medicare deductibles, thus limiting the impact to low-end expenditures, where the case for increasing copayments is strongest. In 1997, the Senate Finance Committee unanimously endorsed a plan to increase the Part B deductible from $100 to $540 for enrollees with incomes of $50,000, rising to a maximum of $2,160 for those with incomes of $100,000 or more. The Committee had been expected to propose income-conditioning for Medicare premiums, but changed course at the last minute, either to increase enrollees' cost consciousness (Clymer 1997) or so that the proposal would look less like a tax (Reischauer 1997). Administratively dubious in any event, since it was supposed to be implemented by the private insurance carriers that oversee Medicare billing, the plan "met pained silence from House Republicans and withering attacks from Democrats" (Clymer 1997), and collapsed politically almost overnight.[7]

Choice of Marginal Tax and Reimbursement Rates. Since a Medicare means test would apply to two intermingled bases (income and Medicare features), it effectively would have two sets of marginal rates. For a given enrollee, the test would potentially affect both how much of an extra dollar of income she got to keep and how much of an extra dollar of healthcare expenditure she was required to bear. In each case, of course, what matters is not the means test's distinctive contribution, but the overall marginal tax rate (MTR) for income and marginal reimbursement rate (MRR) for healthcare expenditure.

On the income side, it is all too easy to overlook the marginal tax rate effects that a given Medicare proposal may have. Thus, consider the short-lived Senate Finance Committee plan to income-condition Part B deductibles. For seniors who were certain to use the entire deductible in any event, the proposal was equivalent to inserting, in the income tax, a $440 "notch" when income increased to $50,000, followed by a 3.24 percent marginal tax rate increase applying solely between $50,000 and $100,000 of income. This ignores the possibility that Medigap coverage would spread the higher deductibles among seniors generally (Reischauer 1997). However, such coverage would be unlikely if the higher deductibles were collected via income tax returns.[8]

Though a system where the marginal tax rate rises and then falls can be defended intellectually,[9] it seems doubtful that anyone in Washington would have proposed it in those terms. Notches and "bubble rates" abound in the fiscal system (the former mainly in transfers and the latter in the income tax), but largely due to a failure to think about them coherently in marginal tax rate terms (Shaviro 1999).

A belief that marginal income tax rates generally should be progressive, rather than declining as income rises, would have clear implications for the design of a Medicare means test. For means-tested premiums and deductibles, it would suggest that the affected amounts should continue rising indefinitely as income increases. Suppose, for example, that one applied the 3.24 percent marginal tax rate in the Senate Finance Committee proposal to Part B premiums, starting at $50,000 (without a notch) and continuing indefinitely. The annual Part B premium ($600 under present law) would be $31,380 for someone with income of $1 million, and $322,980 for someone with income of $10 million.

Would this be as absurd as it sounds? Obviously, it would require making Part B participation mandatory, since no one would voluntarily pay these premiums for the coverage. What is really going on here, however—since a change in the premium has no effect on marginal reimbursement rates for healthcare expenditure—is that seniors' share of the burden of meeting the fiscal gap is being distributed progressively. The proposal would look less absurd if it were redescribed, with no change in its effect on anyone, as simply an income tax rate increase for Medicare enrollees. So perhaps the real problem with allowing the means-tested premium to increase indefinitely (if otherwise good policy) is simply that the fig leaf would cease at some point to offer adequate cover for the enrollees' marginal tax rate increase.[10]

An unlimited increase in deductibles would differ somewhat from such an increase in premiums, since it would cease to affect enrollees once the deductible exceeded their possible healthcare expenditures. Thus, consider an enrollee with $1 million of taxable income, whose deductible would be $29,160 under the Senate Finance Committee's plan if modified to have the 3.24 percent marginal rate continue indefinitely. (Had her income been $10 million, the deductible would have been $320,760.) Medicare would pay for none of her healthcare unless she had significant needs during the year, although even so it would have benefited her ex ante by offering high-end insurance protection. The means test would cost her less than $29,160 if her healthcare expenses were lower. As her income (and thus the deductible) gradually increased past the point where she was likely to incur healthcare expenses, the means test's expected effect on her marginal income tax rate would effectively decline from 3.24 percent to almost zero.

For deductibles and other copayments, unlike premiums, one must consider the effect of means-testing not just on marginal income tax rates, but also on marginal reimbursement rates for healthcare. From this standpoint, there is much to be said in favor of allowing deductibles to increase indefinitely. The paternalism and externality rationales for seeking to ensure that all seniors will get adequate healthcare have ever less weight as means increase, for two reasons. "First, holding constant the illness level and all other influences on use, higher-income and more wealthy seniors will use more care and will spend more than others. Second, a given out-of-pocket expense is more easily budgeted the higher is the person's income" (Pauly 1999b, 78).

Accordingly, if one accepts the case for Medicare means-testing, it makes sense to have Medicare deductibles (perhaps for Part A as well as Part B) rise indefinitely with income. The effect on incentives to seek healthcare at higher income levels gives this approach a significant advantage over charging income-related premiums. This advantage arguably outweighs any disadvantage that one ascribes to the effective decline in marginal tax rate that results from means-testing deductibles.

Income-related deductibles might, however, be inferior to income-related copayments at less than a 100 percent rate, given the evidence that the latter are more efficient. Using income-related copayments rather than deductibles would also ensure that even high-income seniors got some healthcare benefits from Medicare, possibly an advantage if one does not entirely dismiss the political economy argument for protecting its status as a "universal" program.

Choice of Taxpaying Unit. Medicare means-testing ought to apply on a family or household basis, rather than separately to each individual. Since households to some extent pool their resources for distribution among household members without relying solely on who has legal title to what, one cannot accurately judge an individual's material well-being or need without considering the resources of other household members. Thus, Mrs. Bill Gates is unlikely to need Food Stamps even if she has no taxable income and owns no assets.

The existing income tax treatment of households, which ignores couple status except in cases of marriage, is increasingly inadequate in an era when couples do not always marry, and when same-sex couples are not permitted to do so.[11] Certain welfare rules (such as for Food Stamps) define households more broadly in measuring relevant means. However, if income tax returns were used in administering the means test, adoption of the income tax approach to defining couples might be close to unavoidable.

One modification that might result in a more accurate measure of household resources would be to consider children's taxable income in applying the Medicare means test to enrollees. As a practical matter, children's means often affect the healthcare that their parents can afford, since the children may pay for treatment if necessary. Administratively, however, this would be impeded by the concerns underlying tax return confidentiality. Children may not want their parents to know their taxable income. In addition, its implementation would require addressing the "King Lear" problem of children who have the means yet are unwilling to help their parents. Thus, its likely political unfeasibility is not entirely cause for regret.

If we assume that a Medicare means test's sole adjustment for household status is to recognize couples that are eligible to file income tax joint returns, then the question that remains is how it should treat such couples compared to single individuals. An initial point is that the earned income exclusion I suggested earlier should apply separately to each spouse, because decisions whether or not to continue working are made individually. Beyond that, however, matters grow more complicated.

One alternative would be to treat spouses equivalently to single individuals each of whom had half of the couple's income. Thus, if premiums or deductibles for singles start increasing when income reaches X, then for married couples the increase would start when their combined reached $2X$. This would be arithmetically equivalent to "income-splitting," or treating spouses as separate taxpayers except that each got to claim exactly half of their combined income. It would favor married couples with unequal earnings (relative to singles with the same earnings) when the Medicare means test applied progressive marginal rates. However, it would disfavor the married couples when the test was regressive, such as by reason of imposing no further liability above a dollar ceiling.[12]

Alternatively, like the existing income tax, the Medicare means test could use brackets for married couples that were less than double the brackets applying to singles. The 1997 Senate Finance Committee plan followed such an approach. It would have caused spouses' deductibles to increase as their combined income rose from $75,000 to $125,000, rather than $50,000 to $100,000 as with single individuals.

How best to adjust for household status is a complex topic that I cannot fully address here. In general, however, the resources that a couple must have in order to meet their combined needs are likely to be greater, but less than double, than the resources that a single individual needs, due to economies of scale (pertaining, for example, to rent). Less than doubling the brackets may therefore be a reasonable approach, although it is hard to say exactly where one should come out.

This type of approach has recently, and justifiably, encountered serious criticism in the context of the income tax. Complaints emphasize the marriage penalty for many two-earner couples when the rate brackets on joint returns are less than double those on single returns. Concern about these couples' marriage penalties is arguably heightened rather than offset by the fact that the income tax gives one-earner couples a marriage bonus. Moreover, the issue is not just one of unduly favoring one-earner couples and penalizing two-earner couples (with consequences for marriage incentives). An additional problem, which even income-splitting would not solve, is discouraging the secondary earner in a couple (often the wife) from seeking work, since a high marginal tax would apply to her earnings from the first dollar on (McCaffery 1997).

These issues, however, are considerably less applicable to Medicare enrollees. One of the big reasons that the income tax treatment of one-earner versus two-earner couples is so anomalous is that it ignores the economic value of a nonworking spouse's home production, such as in raising children. In effect, the income of a one-earner couple income is undermeasured by excluding the value of the nonworker's services (which really are work). One consequence is that the increase in economic well-being that would result from her going to work is grossly overmeasured by the income tax system, thereby severely discouraging such work (Shaviro 2002).

A Medicare means test would raise less concern about these effects because most enrollees are retired. In addition, I have suggested excluding earned income from the means test up to a dollar ceiling, thus reducing the work disincentive. To be sure, the means test still discourages pre-retirement work and saving, since it is income-based, but this is par for the course when we are taxing income. Finally, as I discuss in chapter 10, Medicare's (and the fiscal system's) bias in favor of one-earner couples can be addressed in other ways.

Summary

Contributions by Medicare enrollees ought to be increased, both to prompt greater cost consciousness at the margin in healthcare expenditure and to help ensure that all living generations contribute to narrowing the fiscal gap. A good starting point would be to address the misuse of Medigap supplemental coverage to undermine Medicare cost-sharing. This could involve a tax on Medigap premiums or a ban on Medigap coverage of Medicare copayments.

Copayments ought to be increased significantly, and also converted from deductibles to require less than 100 percent contributions over a broader range. Doubling the Part B premium, while not affecting cost consciousness, would have the virtues (as well as the vices) of a lump sum tax, and could be rationalized politically as restoring Medicare's original structure.

If contributions by current seniors are to be increased significantly, it is important to allocate the added burden among them in relationship to their ability to pay. Otherwise, seniors with low lifetime incomes or who entered retirement with too little saving might be adversely affected to an unacceptable degree. Thus, Medicare benefits ought to be means-tested.

This inevitably would affect incentives to work and save, but the trade-off between such effects and distributional aims is unavoidable, and would likewise result from making greater use of income and payroll taxes. From a political economy standpoint, means-testing might help to explode the harmful myths that Medicare enrollees only get what they have paid for, and that the program, as it stands, is somehow simultaneously "universal" rather than income related yet highly progressive. In addition, weakening Medicare's political support might not be entirely a bad thing, since at present such support may be too strong in view of the fiscal gap and competing budget priorities.

Means-testing could be based on taxable income with an exclusion for wages up to a ceiling, to reduce the effect on incentives to retire. It might involve an unlimited increase in deductibles or other copayments as taxable income increases, although the rate of increase ought to be kept low in order to keep effective marginal tax rates on seniors in a reasonable range. Alternatively, Medicare benefits (perhaps just up to a ceiling) might be included in taxable income. Adjustments for household status might be keyed to those in the income tax with its joint returns for married couples, despite the serious deficiencies of the current income tax rules.

Paying for Medicare III: Other Financing to Narrow the Fiscal Gap

BENEFIT changes and increased enrollee contributions will almost certainly fall short of eliminating the Medicare (and overall) fiscal gap. Thus, tax increases are highly likely at some point, unpopular though they may be.

The question of how to narrow the fiscal gap through taxes is in some ways not a Medicare question. Suppose that the present value of all expected future Medicare spending declined by $50 trillion but the expected costs of fighting terrorism increased by $50 trillion, leaving the overall fiscal gap unchanged. The issues of efficiency and distribution posed by the choice of taxes to narrow the fiscal gap would be largely unchanged.[1] Still, if we define Medicare reform as requiring that the program be made sustainable, the question of how to raise taxes is unavoidably part of the process. We cannot properly assess benefit cuts or enrollee contribution increases without comparing them to the tax alternatives.

Payroll Taxes and Income Taxes

The Choice between the Two Taxes

The existing payroll tax has several main characteristics. The Medicare portion has a flat rate. Counting the Social Security portion as well, it has a high rate (nominally 15.3 percent) followed by a low rate (2.9 percent). The income tax, by contrast, generally has graduated marginal rates, rising from 0 percent (in light of the standard deduction and personal exemptions) to at least 35 percent, depending on whether the 2001 Tax Act reaches its currently scheduled full phase-in.

As to its base, the payroll tax has more in common with a consumption tax than an income tax. It excludes returns to saving, and would indeed be economically equivalent to a consumption tax if it defined earnings far more broadly. By contrast, the existing income tax reaches returns to saving in some circumstances, albeit that in others it effectively applies consumption tax treatment.[2] Congress has also, to date, mucked around considerably less with the payroll tax base than the income tax base. The former contains far fewer targeted preferences and dispreferences than the latter. Some they have in common, however, such as the exclusion for employer-provided health insurance.

Two other differences between the existing payroll and income taxes are formal only. Payroll tax liability is nominally split 50-50 between employers and workers, whereas the income tax, while subject to employer withholding, is formally described as a tax entirely on the worker. While this nominal split is unlikely to affect economic incidence in the long run (Rosen 1999, 189), it may affect political perceptions, as well as transition incidence when the tax rate unexpectedly changes.[3] In addition, payroll taxes are treated as earmarked for Social Security and Medicare, and thus affect official statements of the programs' trust fund balances.

In principle, each of these various characteristics is independent of all the others. For example, one could make the payroll tax progressive and non-earmarked, while giving the income tax a flat or declining rate and attributing a fixed percentage of its revenues to the trust funds. As a political matter, however, each tax's existing characteristics may tend to remain linked, thus to some extent presenting us with a choice between packages.

Accordingly, the extent to which one favors using the payroll tax rather than the income tax to narrow the Medicare and overall fiscal gap depends on how one views the various components in each package. For example, the more one likes progressivity and taxing returns to saving (two very distinct things),[4] the less should one favor use of the payroll tax. The choice is likely to be only a matter of degree, however. Both taxes are likely to increase, if only to limit the bad news voters can detect in any one place.

Taxation of Employer-Provided Health Insurance

Under both the income tax and the payroll tax, additional revenues can come from base-broadening rather than just rate increases. Base-broadening has the advantage of generally reducing economic distortions (other than the discouragement of work and saving), whereas rate increases enhance them. This is not the place to discuss, say, repealing income tax preferences for owner-occupied housing. However, the income and payroll tax exclusion for employer-provided health insurance has a direct bearing on Medicare. As discussed in chapter 2, it reduces cost consciousness among healthcare consumers generally, encouraging higher treatment norms and discouraging cost-saving technological innovation. Moreover, by habituating voters to the notion that healthcare should be virtually free at the point of purchase, it affects Medicare's political environment by discouraging its redesign as true insurance that emphasizes high-end rather than low-end coverage.

While repeal of the exclusion for employer-provided health insurance is not politically imaginable today, the same is true of any tax increase of the magnitude needed to make a significant dent in the fiscal gap, yet such increases are unlikely to be avoidable forever. One possible way to grease the wheels politically for repeal of the exclusion would be to apply it only to health insurance above a stated dollar value. Such a limitation might even be desirable apart from any political advantages, since it would concentrate the impact of the repeal on overinsurance, as distinct from the decision whether to hold health insurance. Encouraging workers to have basic health insurance may be desirable for the same reasons (paternalism and externalities) that we give seniors Medicare coverage in lieu of cash. However, a recent empirical study suggests that, even if employer-provided health insurance is fully taxed, "the impact on insurance coverage is likely to be small relative to the reduction in spending" (Gruber and Lettau 2000, 33).

Taxing the value of employer-provided health insurance might also, as a political matter, be naturally linked with taxing the value of enrollees' Medicare benefits. The two changes are not identical, since the change for workers would apply to the value of the insurance coverage and that for Medicare enrollees to the healthcare benefits they actually received. (The rationale for this difference is that workers, but not Medicare enrollees under present law, can choose their levels of coverage, thus permitting them to respond to changes in its cost.) The two changes might, however, conveniently be packaged together as parallel provisions to "share the pain."

Bias of the Fiscal System in Favor of One-Earner Married Couples

A further difference between the existing income and payroll taxes is that only the income tax adjusts for household status, such as through joint returns and by allowing personal exemptions for dependents. This makes the income tax the vehicle of choice for addressing Medicare's (and the fiscal system's) bias in favor of one-earner couples.

Use of the payroll tax to compensate for nonworking spouses' free Medicare coverage would not be administratively feasible. However, when married couples file income tax returns, they declare their marital status. In addition, they file W-2 withholding forms that set forth their respective earnings and the payroll taxes (including Medicare taxes) that have been withheld. Income tax returns also are the medium for collecting additional Medicare taxes on earnings that were not subject to employer withholding.

It would not be administratively difficult, therefore, to collect additional Medicare taxes from married couples that had only one significant earner. This might, for example, involve stating a minimum "premium" for the lower earner's coverage, perhaps rising with the spouses' combined income. The premium could be made payable only to the extent that it exceeded the actual Medicare taxes paid by the lower-earning spouse.

Under this proposal, a one-earner couple would pay more Medicare tax than a two-earner couple with the same household income. This outcome may be appropriate, however, since the former couple has greater imputed income if the nonworking spouse has more time to perform household services. Households in which both spouses worked, but one earned a lot more than the other, would not be subject to the extra Medicare tax so long as the low-earner had paid enough Medicare tax in the first place.

One further advantage of this proposal is that it would reduce the influence of the Medicare tax as a marginal factor deterring stay-at-home spouses from going to work. At present, the prospect of paying income and payroll taxes on one's earnings, while also bearing various generally nondeductible expenses (such as for commuting, childcare, and work attire), can reduce a secondary earner's expected after-tax cash gain from going to work to zero or even below. Turning the Medicare tax liability incurred at the job into a mere replacement for the extra "premium" that would have been paid anyway would mitigate this deterrent effect of the fiscal system on work by secondary earners.

The proposal's main disadvantage is that it would impose a marriage penalty. If Ann is supporting Bob and they are not married, no extra payroll tax is owed, yet Bob will still qualify for Medicare coverage at retirement so long as he worked for at least forty quarters. Under the proposal, marriage would raise the couple's Medicare tax liability. Given the general effect of the income tax rewards on one-earner couples, however, they might still have overall marriage bonuses.

Permanent Adoption versus Sunset of the 2001 and 2003 Tax Acts

In 2001, Congress enacted an enormous tax cut, in large part on the premise that contemporary budget surpluses made it feasible and desirable. Taken at face value, this premise was entirely fallacious, given the long-term fiscal gap. "Suppose you were the parent of twin sixteen year-olds, both of whom were highly likely to be going to Ivy League universities in two years without scholarships. If, in the ensuing year, you earned $1,000 more than you spent . . . [w]ould it really make sense . . . to dissipate that $1,000, on the ground that it was an unneeded 'surplus' from the perspective of your annual budget?" (Shaviro 2001a, 1459). The federal government's college-bound twins are, of course, Medicare and Social Security.

Just how little Congress ever needed this excuse became clear in 2003, when huge tax cuts were enacted despite growing budget deficits and the $74 trillion fiscal gap. Here one could not even make the excuse of 2001 that Congress, in the alternative, would have dissipated the surplus through wasteful spending. Even in 2001, however, a great deal of extra spending would have been needed to match the long-term impact of the tax legislation, which, if assumed to be permanent (as its proponents intended), increased the flow fiscal gap by 1.9 percent of the gross domestic product (GDP) (Auerbach, Gale, and Orszag 2002, 16), or the stock fiscal gap by $12.67 trillion.

Tax cut advocates in 2001 and 2003 rightly pointed out that lowering the rates reduces economic distortion and may trigger economic growth. They overlooked, however, the fact that, in light of the fiscal gap, lower rates now imply higher rates in the future. So the issue was really one of rate smoothing, or to what extent tax rates should be level over time, rather than of whether rates should be low or high.

Since (as of mid-2003) the 2001 and 2003 Acts remain subject to sunsets, there is no better place to start in addressing the fiscal gap than by blocking their permanent adoption. Indeed, this would go considerably further toward making our overall fiscal policy (including Medicare) sustainable over the long haul than any imaginable set of Medicare changes with a chance of being adopted over the next few years.

Adoption of a Value-Added Tax

The United States is one of the few economically developed countries without a value-added tax (VAT) as part of its fiscal structure. A VAT is typically a consumption tax, collected, like a retail sales tax, from businesses with respect to their sales to consumers. The big difference between a VAT and a retail sales tax is administrative. Whereas retail sales taxes are meant to apply only to sales from businesses to consumers, VATs apply to interbusiness transactions, where they generally impose a tax liability on the seller while entitling the buyer to a rebate. The net effect may be the same as under a retail sales tax (zero net tax on the participants in an interbusiness transaction), but more of a paper trail is left for audit purposes (Shaviro 2001b, 180).[5]

A number of factors underlie the VAT's appeal in other countries. Governments may consider it an effective money machine because, being paid by businesses even if borne by consumers, it is indirect and potentially less noticed than other taxes. Even if consumers know the VAT rate, they generally do not receive annual statements of their VAT liability, akin to that on an income tax return. Indeed, their VAT payments may not even be stated separately as add-ons to pretax retail prices.

Consumers also do not have to bear the compliance costs of filing tax returns and undergoing audits. And even if, despite all this, voters are approximately as aware of their VAT as their income tax liabilities, governments that levy both may benefit politically from spreading the pain a bit. Better, perhaps, to impose two taxes at 20 percent than one at 40 percent, even if the true burden is identical.

A VAT is almost inevitably a flat-rate tax. The businesses that collect it on their sales to customers cannot be expected to apply one rate on a sale to Bill Gates and another rate on a sale to a factory worker. This need not be a concern, however, if other parts of the fiscal system can be used to achieve the desired overall level of progressivity.

Beyond its merely political advantages, a VAT is genuinely appealing in several respects. Its low administrative cost is not just a political virtue. Moreover, it can be used to shift the fiscal system toward consumption taxation, thus reducing the tax burden on saving. Not all would agree that this is a virtue, but our low national saving rate has evoked much concern.

A final important point raised by the VAT goes to its transition effects when introduced (and subsequently if its rate is changed). In the absence of deliberate transition relief, a consumption-style VAT effectively imposes a one-time wealth tax when it is introduced. An individual who has already accumulated wealth by this time has no way of avoiding it when she spends her wealth (Auerbach and Kotlikoff 1987, 79). She suffers an immediate loss in purchasing power even if her consumption is deferred. Thus, she bears the economic equivalent of a wealth levy even though she may not pay it all for a long time. In effect, the unpaid portion is deferred at a market rate of interest.

This wealth levy has been lauded as economically efficient on the ground that it does not affect incentives to work or save if its adoption is unanticipated and taxpayers believe that it will never be levied again (79). I have elsewhere disagreed on two main grounds. First, people would likely see the VAT coming, leading to discouragement of work and saving before its adoption. Second, they would anticipate its being imposed again (such as through rate increases), since the logic of claiming it will be imposed just once is infinitely repeatable (Shaviro 2000b, 184–85). This does not, however, mean that the ostensibly one-time wealth levy from adopting a VAT is a bad idea. It merely indicates that we cannot get something in distributional terms for nothing in efficiency terms. Taxing work and saving tends to discourage work and saving, no matter how solemn the accompanying pledges never to do it again. Thus, the wealth levy aspect of introducing a VAT, just like the steady-state application of an income, payroll, or consumption tax, has a familiar efficiency price.

The burden imposed by the wealth levy would at least be distributed progressively. Moreover, it would reach current seniors, who are still consuming even if no longer working, and who would largely escape any burden from raising income or payroll taxes to address the fiscal gap. Each of these distributional results might be harder to achieve explicitly and directly than as a by-product of adopting a tax that, as a flat-rate tax on consumption, is widely viewed as regressive.

A major reason why a VAT has not yet been adopted in the United States is that, in our relatively antitax political environment, its character as a potential money machine is considered a vice rather than a virtue. This may change, however, if seniors' entitlement benefits come to be seen as imminently at risk. "Save Social Security and Medicare" might prove a sufficiently potent battle cry to overcome voters' reluctance to give Congress a potent new revenue tool that, once in place, might prove harder than the income tax to restrain. However, the adoption of a VAT, like any other tax increase that was touted as a device to save the entitlement programs, would raise the question of how to ensure that the revenues really would be used as promised. Revenue earmarking is inherently a tricky proposition, because, unless Clown family accounting-style compliance is thought sufficient, the question is not really where the specific dollars at issue end up going. Rather, it is how the extra revenues affect Congress's overall tax and spending decisions.

Suppose, for example, that a tax increase raised $10 billion per year, earmarked for Medicare, and that all of the actual dollars from the enactment were duly used to pay Medicare bills. If Medicare would otherwise have gotten a different $10 billion, and Congress responded to the tax increase by loosening up its pork barrel spending to the tune of $10 billion per year, then the earmarking claim would be true only in the most trivial sense.

The difficulty of ensuring real, as opposed to merely nominal, earmarking of revenues provides a major challenge for anyone who wants to narrow the fiscal gap by generating advance funding for Medicare's expected future liabilities. Since the government cannot bind itself (unlike a private firm that can guarantee its pension commitments by placing funds in trust or escrow), the best it can do is create institutional circumstances that increase the political likelihood of real earmarking over a multiyear period. The question of how to backstop earmarking is therefore a critical part of seeking to pay for Medicare through tax increases that anticipate the explosion in expenditures.

Changes in Medicare Accounting Conventions

Two main methods have been discussed for using Medicare accounting conventions to discourage Congress from cutting other taxes or raising other spending in response to a tax increase that was aimed at narrowing the fiscal gap. The first is to modify the official definition or use of the Medicare Trust Funds. The second is officially (whether or not substantively) to create Medicare medical savings accounts.

Medicare Trust Funds

The current definition and use of the Medicare Trust Funds involves two arguable anomalies. First, only the Part A Trust Fund accomplishes even nominal earmarking. While it ostensibly reserves the Medicare portion of the payroll tax to pay for Part A benefits and nothing else, Part B has no such mechanism. By definition, the Part B Trust Fund cannot be exhausted, since it is treated as using whatever general revenues are needed, rather than a dedicated financing source.

The second anomaly involves computation of the official "on-budget" surplus or deficit. By law, the revenues and expenditures of the Social Security Trust Fund are excluded from the on-budget measure, though not from the official "unified" measure. No such exclusion applies to Medicare, even though its Part A Trust Fund is functionally similar to the Social Security Trust Fund.

Neither of these anomalies has any obvious rationale. Rather, they appear simply to reflect accidents of history. Part A but not Part B was given dedicated financing as a by-product of Medicare's 1965 legislative history. As for the on-budget computation, Social Security was excluded in order "to stress the need to provide independent, sustainable funding for Social Security in the long term, and to show the extent to which the rest of the budget has relied on annual Social Security surpluses to make up for its own shortfall" (Office of Management and Budget 2002, 34). Medicare has no less need for sustainable long-term funding than Social Security. And Part A of Medicare, no less than Social Security, ostensibly has independent funding that is currently in surplus (despite its long-term shortfall) and therefore helps to offset any measured shortfall in the rest of the budget. It just so happens, however, that Congress did not move Part A off-budget when it did so with Social Security, perhaps because Medicare's long-term financing problems were attracting less attention at the time.

The question of real interest, however, is not whether these anomalies are logically defensible. Rather, it is what effect correcting them would have on Congress's propensity to widen the fiscal gap. After all, the trust funds and annual budget computations are arbitrary no matter how we define them. Rather than offering economically coherent measures of government policy, they are merely crude devices to backstop earmarking and nudge Congress in the direction of putting fiscal policy on a sustainable path. Along these lines, there are indeed arguments both for extending "real" trust fund treatment to Part B of Medicare and for moving at least Part A off-budget.

Extending "Real" Trust Fund Treatment to Part B. The Part A Trust Fund potentially serves two constructive purposes in encouraging legislative restraint. It discourages the enactment of new Part A benefits that would hasten its exhaustion, and it may help dramatize the adverse long-term fiscal picture. Similar purposes might be served by subjecting Part B benefits to a similar hurdle.

Suppose, for example, that Parts A and B were officially combined in a single trust fund, with Part B's dedicated financing being defined as a fixed percentage of income tax revenues. At present, the annual general revenue contribution to finance Part B is about 6 percent of individual and corporate income tax revenues. One could therefore provide that 6 percent of these revenues would be treated as dedicated Medicare tax financing. The Part A Trust Fund, which now would cover all of Medicare, would henceforth be treated both as increased by these revenues and as decreased by Part B expenditures. The result, if nothing else changed, would be swifter exhaustion of the Trust Fund (as Part B expenditure grows faster than the income tax) with a consequent need for congressional action to prevent a benefit cut-off (which now would extend to Part B as well as Part A).

Moving Medicare Off-Budget. If Part A of Medicare were treated as off-budget, the on-budget measure of the surplus or deficit would be made to look worse until such time as Part A started running its own annual deficits (currently projected to happen after 2015). The effect of doing the same with Part B, once it had been turned into a "real" trust fund (and whether or not it was combined with Part A) would depend on how the dedicated revenues were defined. For example, if Congress set them at 7 percent of income tax proceeds—thereby causing the Medicare Trust Fund to look longer-lived—the effect would be to make the on-budget picture, which now excluded these revenues, look worse. Or if Congress low-balled the official measure of dedicated Part B revenues at 5 percent of income tax proceeds, it would make the on-budget picture look better but the Medicare Trust Fund look worse.[6]

Moving Medicare off-budget would matter only insofar as political actors treated the on-budget measure as significant. It would thus be little different from reviving the "lockbox" idea, which held, while in vogue during 2000 and most of 2001, that the unified budget surplus should not sink below the Social Security plus Medicare Part A surpluses. For much of 2001, the Bush administration faced significant political pressure to show that its tax cut proposals would not lead to violation of the lockbox norm. There was even widespread congressional support for budget legislation that would have purported to require compliance with it. Then the World Trade Center Towers fell on September 11, 2001, and the lockbox instantaneously evaporated from American political discourse. The new consensus, holding that even immense and ever-growing budget deficits were now completely acceptable, went beyond merely exempting the costs of fighting terrorism from the limitation. Somehow, the collapse of the Towers—even though it worsened the long-term fiscal picture by indicating a greater need to fight terrorism—made it newly permissible to increase, say, farm subsidies without regard to the lockbox.

The fate of the lockbox helps show that one should not be overly sanguine about the capacity of accounting conventions to constrain the political process. Indeed, even if a given accounting convention is enshrined in law, like the Social Security and Medicare Part A Trust Funds or the definition of "on-budget," Congress is likely in the end to do what it wants unless the convention has a grip on the public mind, which cannot be legislated. Still, such steps as adding Part B of Medicare to the Part A Trust Fund and taking Medicare off-budget seem more likely to help than hurt, and thus are worth taking unless they crowd out other changes that would accomplish more.

Medicare Medical Savings Accounts

The difficulty of constraining Congress from dissipating any new tax revenues that were meant to help meet future Medicare liabilities has led some commentators to endorse what looks like a fundamentally different approach. This would involve the use of Medicare medical savings accounts (MSAs)—perhaps, but not necessarily, in connection with privatizing Medicare's health insurance coverage to be offered by competing private firms.

Privatizing Medicare's health insurance coverage—which would be a real change, not an accounting change—might conveniently involve the use of vouchers. This alone would not require changing the government's accounting for Medicare. A privatized Medicare might be reported the same way as the existing system in our fiscal accounts, with voucher expenditures simply replacing direct payments to healthcare providers. However, leading advocates of privatization, who want Medicare to be prefunded whether it is privatized or not, favor the use of Medicare MSAs mainly as a device to discourage Congress from regarding the funds as available for its other purposes.

In a "true" MSA, the amount that you mandatorily or voluntarily contribute, and your investment returns on this amount, might be expected to determine what benefits you get at the end. Indeed, such a relationship between contributions, investment returns, and benefits might be imposed even in a "progressive privatization" plan, with transfers from high-earners' to low-earners' accounts, like the one I have elsewhere proposed for Social Security (Shaviro 2000a, 152–56).

However, leading proponents of Medicare MSAs recognize, whether out of conviction or as a political constraint, that "the basic benefits of Medicare . . . [must] be equal for all and independent of past earnings" (Feldstein 1999, 10). Accordingly, they have proposed ostensible Medicare MSAs in which, for the members of a given age cohort, there would be no relation between contributions and deposits, and no individual investment discretion. For example, all participants might be subject to a flat-rate payroll tax, leading at year's end to a deposit in each participant's account for the average amount of payroll tax paid. Only for an entire age cohort, therefore, would account deposits match tax contributions (Feldstein 1999,10; Rettenmaier and Saving 2000, 125).

If I make mandatory contributions of X, have no investment discretion, and end up with an MSA of amount Y that is unrelated to X and must be used to purchase health insurance coverage, then what role is the MSA really playing? The government might as well simply have taxed me X and then handed me a voucher for Y when I reached age sixty-five. The political influence of accounting conventions aside, it makes no difference that the government has chosen to describe this money as belonging to me via my individual account rather than to a collective trust fund. Indeed, the main difference is political and perceptual even if the money is actually deposited in a bank account that is formally in my name (but that I cannot access other than to pay for a voucher).

Accordingly, it is fair to describe this use of Medicare MSAs as merely a change in government accounting conventions (along with the change in generational policy if each age cohort pays in full for its own retirement healthcare). The proponents hope that, by persuading Congress to adopt a description of the revenues at issue as belonging to people's private accounts, they will be able to dissuade it from subsequently counting these revenues when it decides how much to spend on government programs generally. This in turn, they hope, will increase national saving (relative to the use of collective trust funds) if Congress would otherwise have spent the money on consumption goods.

Medicare MSAs could also be created without a tax increase by diverting (if that is not too strong a word for a mere accounting change) existing tax revenues, such as those from the Medicare payroll tax. Once again, the aim would be to reduce government spending by causing these revenues to be otherwise excluded from the government's books of account.

In sum, there is less than meets the eye to this use of Medicare MSAs, which merely takes the lockbox or off-budget idea for the Medicare Trust Funds a step further. Nonetheless, the proponents may be right that, as accounting changes go, it would be more effective. The claim to be establishing Medicare MSAs (without necessarily changing or increasing benefits) might be especially helpful as political cover for the enactment of a tax increase that was meant to help make future benefits affordable. For example, a newly enacted VAT might be disbursed to Medicare MSAs that, at retirement, would be used to help fund people's existing benefits. Still, one should not exaggerate voters' naïveté and capacity to be duped (albeit in a good cause) by an accounting change of this kind. If they do not want to narrow the fiscal gap, whether because they misunderstand it or are unconcerned about future generations, they most likely will insist that their elected representatives give them what they want.

Summary

The main taxes that are likely to be used in narrowing the fiscal gap are the existing income and payroll taxes and a consumption-style VAT. If the former two are stable "packages" that cannot be recombined in new ways, one's choice between them should largely depend on weighing the income tax's greater progressivity against its more pockmarked tax base and discouragement of saving. The political choice between the two taxes may also be influenced by the fact that the payroll tax is nominally half-paid by employers (although this should not affect its incidence beyond the short term) and has traditionally been credited to the Social Security and Medicare Part A Trust Funds.

The value of employer-provided health insurance should be included in both tax bases, at least to the extent in excess of a floor amount. The income tax should also be used to address Medicare's bias in favor of one-earner married couples. This might involve stating a minimum "premium" for the lower earner's coverage that would be payable, as an add-on, to the extent that it exceeded that individual's actual Medicare taxes paid. Other income tax preferences should also be repealed in lieu of increasing the rates. In addition, the tax cuts from the 2001 and 2003 Acts ought generally to be reversed on the ground that they are unsustainable given the long-term picture.

The adoption of a VAT, in addition to the existing income and payroll taxes, would have several advantages. It is an administratively simple tax, albeit not a progressive one. Its transition incidence as an ostensibly one-time wealth levy that would reach current seniors to the extent of their ability to pay (as measured by wealth) may also be appealing, even if one rejects the claim that the transition tax is lump-sum and nondistortionary.

Any effort to narrow the fiscal gap and accumulate funds to pay for future Medicare benefits raises the question of how to prevent these funds from being dissipated. Since Congress cannot be legally compelled to shut its eyes to the buildup of funds as it makes other fiscal decisions, the best one can do is try to nudge it in that direction with accounting conventions. Within the current structure, one possibility is to combine the Part A and Part B Trust Funds, with Part B revenues being defined as a fixed percentage (say, 6 percent) of income tax revenues. A second possible accounting change is to move Medicare, like Social Security, off-budget. However, these changes, while unlikely to hurt, might not help much.

A more seemingly radical accounting change would be to define certain taxes paid as contributions to Medicare MSAs. Taxes paid would not have to match deposits made, except perhaps for an entire age cohort. People's ownership of their MSAs would be fictional if that they had no investment discretion and were required to use the funds at retirement to pay for the same benefits that they would have gotten in any event. Yet Medicare MSAs might help grease the wheels politically for the adoption of a VAT that was used to fund them, in addition to discouraging dissipation of the revenues.

Conclusions and Predictions

How Should Medicare Change?

THERE is no perfect plan to "save" and improve Medicare by narrowing the fiscal gap and altering its insurance design. Any comprehensive proposal to this effect, even if its enactment were not a fantasy, would involve hard and contestable choices, as to which opinions may reasonably differ, along with substantial empirical uncertainty. Nonetheless, I have tried in this book to offer, in broad brushstrokes, a general agenda for changing Medicare. My main suggestions have included the following:

1. Reduce Medicare's low-end coverage of routine expenditures, and use replace deductibles with lesser copayments that extend over a broader range.

2. Provide prescription drug and catastrophic care coverage without increasing the overall value (net of premiums and copayments) of Medicare coverage.

3. Impose a tax on Medigap coverage of Medicare copayments, or else bar such coverage altogether.

4. Make copayments income-related, so that their percentage and/or their range increases with taxable income, which for this purpose would be reduced by an exclusion for wages up to a threshold amount. An alternative approach is to treat the value of Medicare benefits received, perhaps up to a ceiling, as taxable income.

5. To the extent that income tax increases are needed, use base-broadening in lieu of rate increases to the extent possible. The value of employer-provided health insurance, at least to the extent in excess of a threshold amount, should be included in the income and payroll tax bases. One-earner couples should pay extra premiums for their joint Medicare coverage, to be collected on income tax returns through an income-related minimum Medicare tax on the lower earner. And the fiscally imprudent tax cuts of 2001 and 2003 should be scaled back as soon as possible.

6. Enact a consumption-style VAT without transition relief for old wealth.

7. Use accounting rules to discourage Congress from dissipating the net revenue from tax increases that are meant to help meet future Medicare liabilities. This could involve combining the Part A and Part B Trust Funds (with a fixed percentage of income tax revenues being treated as dedicated to the latter), and revising the official on-budget measure of the deficit or surplus to exclude Medicare. A seemingly more radical accounting change involves describing certain taxes paid as contributions to Medicare medical savings accounts (MSAs). All members of a given age cohort would get the same contribution even if they paid different tax amounts. Medicare MSAs would be treated as helping pay for the coverage, although this would not necessarily imply any change in structure.

8. Attempt to realize cost savings by modifying Medicare's current fee for service structure. While managed care has had disappointing results as applied to workers under age sixty-five, this may reflect the political and legal obstacles to imposing rationing. However, the character of any such changes lie beyond the subject matter of this book.

What Is Most Likely to Happen?

As a commentator with academic tenure and no political aspirations, I can readily offer unpopular proposals like those above without concern about the professional repercussions. By contrast, a candidate for public office who advanced them would likely be committing political suicide. Few if any of the proposals are apt to be enacted or even seriously considered any time soon.

In making the proposals, I have sporadically tried to address problems of political feasibility. I did not, however, make current political feasibility a prerequisite. Doing so would have required declining to address Medicare's problems in a serious fashion. Today's political reality is simply too much at odds with long-term economic reality for a set of Medicare reform proposals to be both responsible and currently enactable. I have generally thought it better to be politically unrealistic than irresponsible or blind—not just out of aesthetic preference (though partly that), but also on the view that this reflects a proper division of labor. Those with stronger Washington policymaking ties are better situated to navigate from where we are in the maze, but less inclined to look far ahead or consider the maze's layout from above.

Unfortunately, current political debate in Washington—even though many policymakers know better—seems premised on widening, not narrowing, the fiscal gap. Enormous tax cuts and proposed benefit enhancements are the order of the day. If anything, politicians' awareness of our long-term fiscal problems has only made them compete the more reck-lessly to get what they can for their constituencies or policy views today, lest someone else get through the door before it slams shut.

Beyond the immense complexity of the issues, there are three core po-litical problems to reforming Medicare. Future generations cannot yet vote. Current workers are less politically well organized than seniors and the healthcare industry. Finally, it is hard to make current workers enor-mously enthusiastic about a forced saving program, whereby they sacri-fice today so that their healthcare options upon retirement will be better. Workers today may have noticed, moreover, that older age cohorts got free benefits without the sky falling. This naturally inclines one to assume that we can just continue passing the burden forward. Similar reasoning ("It worked yesterday, so it will work tomorrow") underlay the Internet bubble and day-trading craze of the late 1990s.

What, then, should we expect to happen? This is the subject of consid-erable disagreement, even among those who recognize that the currently announced fiscal policy of the U.S. government does not add up. Under a pessimistic view, if you look ahead to 2030, "[y]ou see a government in desperate trouble—raising taxes to unprecedented levels, making drastic benefit cuts, cutting domestic government spending to the bone, borrow-ing far beyond its capacity to repay, and printing lots of money to 'meet' its bills. You also see major tax evasion, high and rising rates of inflation, a growing informal sector, a rapidly depreciating currency, large capital outflows, and more people leaving than entering the country. In short, you see an America in 2030 that looks a lot like Russia circa today" (Kotlikoff 2001, 5).

Others see considerably less cause for concern. Since the fiscal gap re-flects an imbalance within our currently stated or discerned long-term policies, all it necessarily implies is that the statements will have to change. I earlier gave the example of the alimony agreement in which the high-earning spouse is supposed to turn over 30 percent of his income each year, while the low-earner is supposed to get 50 percent. While such an agreement cannot be implemented, both of the spouses should do fine in the end so long as the income that is being split remains high. Much can go wrong, however, by reason of the unfeasible agreement. For example, they might collectively spend 120 percent of their available income, or destroy their economic prospects by battling over who gets what.

Translated back to Medicare, the potential adverse consequences are as follows. Current generations may spend more than they ought to given the claims of future generations, and allocate too little of their lifetime spending to retirement. This may lead them unable to afford retirement health-care that had the potential to help them a great deal. In addition, belated recognition of the fiscal gap may encourage hasty, last-minute adoption of foolish policies in response to crises that should have been easy to antici-pate. Still, this does not make us Russia circa 2000, and even insofar as it does we may suffer in style to the extent that we have grown wealthier.

What, more specifically, should we expect to happen? While the future is inevitably opaque, here is a forecast. The next few years may see the adoption of policies that widen the fiscal gap, including the enactment of unfunded prescription drug benefits that keep getting larger through a po-litical bidding process. By 2010–20, however, the entitlement programs' fiscal prospects will look grave enough to prompt significant tax increases that are now unthinkable. These will include the enactment of a VAT that is officially earmarked to one or both of the entitlements, because the lure of a dedicated money machine will have grown too great to pass up.

Medigap will be addressed at some point, because cross-subsidization is so hard to defend, but the impact of the change will be unduly deferred. Copayments will increase and the Medicare eligibility age be postponed, though again with a deferred effective date. Explicit means-testing within Medicare is unlikely, however, because it "concentrates costs on a politi-cally active group [that] regards such a move as an abandonment of Medi-care's social insurance contract" (Oberlander 2003, 168). And Medicare will continue to misdirect its insurance coverage toward the low end as opposed to the high end, since the 1988 catastrophic care catastrophe, along with what it revealed about political preferences, make that issue unlikely to be revisited.

Inflation will be used to narrow the fiscal gap, and legal changes made to help it do so. These might include eliminating or reducing the indexing of income tax rate brackets and Social Security benefits. Medicare will benefit fiscally from inflation because it permits payments to providers to decline in real terms without declining nominally. Indeed, doctors will drop out of Medicare in increasing numbers as its payment fees shrink rel-ative to those that patients with the cash are willing to pay. One is entitled to hope, however, that policymakers have learned (and remember) enough to ensure that we stop short of runaway or hyperinflation.

With all these measures falling short of meeting the fiscal gap, it is hard to see a politically realistic alternative to healthcare rationing (for workers as well as Medicare enrollees). Healthcare providers will be squeezed a bit on their sunk-cost investments despite their political influence, reducing subsequent investment in the field (in terms of human capital as well as technology). Queuing and delay in receiving treatment will be the chief rationing tools of choice, since they dodge the awkwardness of explicitly denying care. And the disparity between healthcare for the rich and the poor will grow, involving associated amenities as well as the care itself.

Lest this picture sound too grim, however, even the poorer people who get the worst care may still, in absolute terms, be getting better care than anyone gets today. Despite rationing, they will derive some benefit from procedures that do not now exist. And if material life as a whole turns out to be worse in absolute terms, it will be for reasons (such as terrorism, environmental degradation, and newly disease-resistant germs) that have little to do with Medicare or the fiscal gap.

Our fiscal problems have their roots in two related, technologically driven shocks to the system: increasing life expectancy and the development of costly yet valuable new medical treatments. If only these had not happened, the United States might be in long-term fiscal balance. We would on average die sooner after having been sicker while we lived, but at least our announced fiscal policies would add up.

Obviously, it is better to be healthier, live longer, and choose poorly given the available opportunities than to reverse all three. Still, our political myopia is cause for regret if it ultimately leads to reduced economic growth and unnecessary levels of healthcare rationing and wealth-related treatment disparity. Being (we hope) in most respects fortunate to live today, rather than in the past, is no excuse for squandering opportunities to make things better in the future.

NOTES

Chapter One

1. Medicare also serves disabled individuals and end-stage renal patients, but throughout this book I leave to one side the distinct issues that are raised by these areas of coverage.

Chapter Two

1. Medicare's definition of what constitutes inpatient hospital care is quite broad. It "includes costs of a semi-private room, meals, regular nursing services, operating and recovery rooms, intensive care, inpatient prescription drugs, laboratory tests, X-rays, psychiatric hospitals, inpatient rehabilitation, and long-term care (LTC) hospitalization when medically necessary, as well as other medically necessary services and supplies provided in the hospital" (Hoffman, Klees, and Curtis 2000).

2. Among the items included in Part B coverage are services provided by physicians and surgeons, along with those provided by certain nonphysicians such as clinical social workers and nurse practitioners; emergency room and outpatient clinic services; certain home healthcare; laboratory tests; X-rays; physical and occupational therapy and speech pathology; radiation therapy, kidney dialysis and transplants, and certain heart and liver transplants; wheelchairs and prosthetic devices; and a few drugs (such as hepatitis B vaccines) that cannot be self-administered (Hoffman, Klees, and Curtis 2000).

3. By one recent estimate, Medicare's HMO enrollees would have cost the system 6 percent less than what it paid the HMOs had they remained in its FFS program (Brown et al. 1993). Another recent study placed overpayment at 8 percent (Riley et al. 1996).

4. Gruber and Lettau (2000, 31) estimate that repeal of the various tax exclusions for employer-provided health insurance would increase its median tax price by over 50 percent. Thus, for example, insurance that at present costs the parties $1 after-tax would cost more than $1.50. Putting it the other way around, the exclusions lower the price by more than a third, or from over $1.50 to just $1. One small criticism of the Gruber–Lettau calculation is that it disregards the possibility that inclusion for payroll tax purposes, by increasing the measure of career earnings on which Social Security benefits are based, would to some extent result in a wage subsidy offsetting the wage tax. See Shaviro 2000a, 13–14.

5. Solely under the income tax, medical expenses directly by the consumer are deductible in limited circumstances. First, they are allowed as an itemized deduction to the extent in excess of 10 percent of the taxpayer's adjusted gross income for the year. This, of course, offers no benefit to most people who incur only routine expenses. Second, under employer "cafeteria plans," workers may to a limited extent set aside funds, deducted from their paychecks, that can then be used to meet medical expenses. The amounts set aside, however, are subject to an annual "use-it-or-lose it" rule, with the consequence that they must be kept relatively low if one does not want to risk wasting or forfeiting them.

6. Officially, the rate is 15.3 percent (the sum of 7.65 percent rates imposed on both the employer and the employer), and the 2003 ceiling was $87,000. The combined rate is really

only 14.2 percent, however, because the employer share is excluded from the payroll tax base. As an illustration, suppose that your final 2003 paystub put you right at the official ceiling with earnings of $87,000 and that you therefore, at a 7.65 percent nominal rate, owed payroll taxes of $6,655. The employer's total outlay is $87,000 plus its own liability of $6,655, for a total of $93,655. The combined payroll taxes of $13,310 are about 14.2 percent of this amount.

7. The 2.9 percent rate above the ceiling is likewise an official rate (composed of 1.45 percent pieces paid by employers and employees alike) that similarly should be adjusted for exclusion from the tax base of the employer share. However, the adjusted rate of 2.859 percent (2.9/101.45) still rounds off to 2.9 percent.

8. The income tax has a graduated rate structure that rises with income, whereas the Medicare portion of the payroll tax has a flat rate structure. Initially (like the rest of the payroll tax to this day), it had a zero rate about a relatively modest income level. In addition, the income tax, unlike the payroll tax, includes returns to saving that tend to be proportionately higher among the more affluent.

9. Prior to the 1993 legislation, 50 percent of the Social Security benefits received by people with income above a specified threshold had been subject to income taxation, with the resulting revenues being treated as contributions to the Social Security Trust Fund. In 1993 the percentage was increased to 85 percent, under the provision that the revenues from this increase would be treated as contributions to the Part A Medicare trust fund.

Chapter Three

1. To be sure, we could just as easily call the taxpayers the losers from the inefficiency if we posit that they would give me $10 of value in any event, and thus that offering me cash would enable them to save $70.

2. The Medigap revenue estimates may nonetheless include income effects. By eliminating cost sharing at the margin, Medigap coverage in effect makes its purchasers wealthier in states of the world where satisfying their medical needs would have required copayments that were above, rather than below, the expected level. People who could not have afforded the higher copayments may therefore spend more on average, once they have Medigap coverage, even if they never seek treatment that is worth less to them than cash in the amount of the treatment's cost.

3. These incentive effects would be offset to the extent that an increase in earnings (or in payroll taxes paid) implied an increase in expected benefits. Social Security actually has such a correlation given the mechanics of its benefit formula (which increases with covered lifetime earnings). This correlation, however, may not be well understood (Shaviro 2000a, 12–13; Kotlikoff and Sachs 1997, 17). In the case of Medicare, evidence from McClellan and Skinner (1997) that I discuss later in this chapter, to the effect that Medicare benefits are positively correlated with lifetime income, might have similar implications to the Social Security benefit formula if generally understood. Suppose, however, that some independent variable causes the observed correlation between lifetime income and high Medicare expenditure. In that case, expected Medicare benefits would not offset the incentive effects of the payroll tax even assuming full understanding by workers.

4. This scenario assumes relatively modest growth in per capita Medicare expenditures and life expectancy. Higher growth rates would increase benefits' cash value but also require tax increases that even people born as early as 1960 may be likely to bear.

5. A further distributional effect of income-related differences in life expectancy is that poorer individuals are more likely to die before they reach age sixty-five, at which point they

have paid taxes but not received any Medicare benefits. This is left out of the McClellan–Skinner study, because it focuses on expenditure for those who reach age sixty-five.

6. Yet another possible distributional effect of Medicare is its increasing compensation for healthcare workers, who tend to be highly paid. Considering this factor might cause Medicare to look more regressive still (McClellan and Skinner 1997, 11–12).

Chapter Four

1. In earlier work (Shaviro 2000a, 29), I used the same equation to describe Social Security.

2. An identical point about the theoretical offset between income effects and retirement effects, so far as effects on national saving are concerned, is commonplace in discussion of Social Security (Shaviro 2000a, 86).

3. Returns above the frontier are available only as limited special opportunities (for example, if Bill Gates in 1985 asks you to invest in Microsoft and you realize what a goldmine it will prove to be). Those below the frontier are to be avoided if you can correctly identify them, since by definition you could match the expected return with less risk, or else match the risk with a greater expected return.

Chapter Five

1. One key difference between Harsanyi's and Rawls' treatment of the veil of ignorance is that Harsanyi argues for maximizing expected utility (which leads to a utilitarian view of social welfare) while Rawls adopts an ad hoc assumption of infinite risk aversion, suggesting that the relevant circumstances of the worst-off person in the society matter infinitely more to the observer behind the veil than those of anyone else.

2. For limited instances of addressing income risk through private arrangements, consider fixed annuities that eliminate investment risk, or the fact that some universities and professional schools offer student loans with repayment terms that depend on how much the borrower subsequently earns.

3. On the availability heuristic, which may cause people to underestimate low-probability events not within their recent experience, see, e.g, Tversky and Kahneman 1974, 1127. On optimism bias, see, e.g., Weinstein 1980.

Chapter Six

1. Since Samuelson was writing before the modern era of financial innovation, there seemed no need to ask a question that might naturally arise today: whether private financial markets could develop instruments that would pay off at the rate of productivity growth, and thus whether government intervention was needed to close a gap in these markets.

2. Samuelson (1958, 471–74) offers a similar analysis. However, he discusses it in relationship to the empirical proposition that, under specified conditions, an "economy has an equilibrium market rate of interest exactly equal to its biological percentage growth rate" (472), rather than from a social insurance standpoint.

Chapter Seven

1. See Kotlikoff 2001 at 8 and 18, arguing that government forecasts both of long-term productivity growth and of the rate of future Medicare spending growth are too optimistic.

2. There would be considerably less reason to object to a seventy-five-year measurement period if the years outside the window had no expected systematic direction. They are expected, however, to involve very large deficits in the absence of policy change.

3. See Kotlikoff 2001, at 11–12; Auerbach, Gale, and Orszag 2002, at 7–8. Even within the short term, the CBO view implies that discretionary spending would fall by about 20 percent relative to GDP and 9 percent per capita by 2010.

4. See Auerbach, Gale, and Orszag 2002, 7. Similarly misleading was Congress's failure in the 2001 Act to account for scaling back the alternative minimum tax (AMT), which was projected, in light of the 2001 changes, to reach more than 35 million taxpayers, or about one-third of the total, by 2010 (10). No matter what one might think of this outcome as a matter of policy, it is extremely unlikely to be allowed to happen given the AMT's complexity. See Shaviro 2001a.

5. Keeping constant the debt to GDP ratio is reasonable under the assumption that debt cannot keep growing relative to GDP. Moreover, even if it did grow in relative terms, paying interest on the added debt forever would be mathematically equivalent to paying off that debt. This second consideration also explains why it would make no difference if the fiscal gap were measured under the assumption that even the government debt must ultimately be paid off.

6. The present value of a fixed perpetuity of $\$X$ is $\$X/\underline{R}$. Thus, at a 5 percent interest rate, a $\$5$ perpetuity has a present value of $\$100$, the amount needed to pay that amount annually forever. Where the perpetuity grows, however, the denominator in the equation is the excess of the discount rate over the growth rate, since future payments decline in present value only to the extent of that excess.

7. This assumes conforming changes to the alternative minimum tax, as discussed above.

8. This estimate reflects using a 3 percent discount rate and assuming 1.5 percent annual GDP growth. Accordingly, GDP ten years from now is assumed to be $\$11.6$ trillion, rather than $\$10$ trillion.

Chapter Eight

1. Aaron argues that comprehensive government regulation is necessary, given how managed care as well as fee for service arrangements are compromised by consumers' inability to assess their own healthcare needs.

2. One also should not be too swayed by the commonplace, but misleading, observation that the millions of Americans who newly found themselves in managed care in the 1990s did not freely choose it, but rather had it thrust upon them. To be sure, this may have been many people's subjective experience when their employers changed the roster of available health insurance options to eliminate fee-for-service coverage. But there is no reason to doubt that profit-minded insurers would offer this coverage if it could be sold at a sufficient premium to cover the expected costs. Nor is there reason to doubt that profit-minded employers would let their workers pay the higher premiums, through adjustments to their cash compensation, if the workers wanted the coverage enough. So people under age sixty-five (unless their preferences were being wildly misjudged by those with an incentive to get it right) really did choose to switch to managed care, just as someone who really likes to drink Dom Perignon might nonetheless choose draft beers given her budget and market prices.

3. Recent proposals to bring competitive private supply, with a managed-care-like structure, to Medicare include the following, all dating from 1999: (a) the Breaux–Thomas plan, developed by Senator John Breaux and Representative Bill Thomas in connection with their work as cochairs of the Bipartisan Commission on the Future of Medicare; (b) the Breaux–Frist plan, which proposed legislation setting forth a modified version of Breaux–Thomas, was introduced in the Senate by Senators Breaux and Bill Frist; and (c) then-President Clin-

ton's "competitive defined benefit" plan. See McClellan 2000b, 28–31 for a concise description.

4. See, e.g., Dowd, Feldman, and Christianson 1996; Study Panel on Capitation and Choice 1998; Jones 1998; Robinson and Powers 1998; Vogel 1999; and Moon 2000.

Chapter Nine

1. A means test might, however, have less deterrent effect on work and saving than a straightforward means tax if enrollees were prone to underestimating their likely healthcare expenditures.

2. Demogrants, or uniform cash benefits that are financed by progressive taxes, may be used to provide transfers to the poor without creating excessive effective marginal tax rates at the point where one starts to escape from poverty. See Shaviro 1999.

3. The basic reason for this equivalence between wage and consumption taxation is that wages are ultimately spent on consumption. Even if saved indefinitely, their value comes from the purchasing power that they represent. Imposing a tax at the point of consumption is therefore equivalent in present value terms to imposing it when the wages are earned, since a consumption tax is neutral as to the time of consumption. See Auerbach and Kotlikoff 1987, 57–58; Shaviro 2000b, 171–73. One should keep in mind, however, that the equivalence depends on defining "wages" to include all real, risk-adjusted returns to investment that exceed the ordinary return to waiting. Thus, for example, it would include (unlike the existing payroll tax) all of the extraordinary appreciation that has accrued to Bill Gates over the last few decades from his owning Microsoft shares.

4. The underlying intuition is based on the fact that an asset's value equals the present value of all the net cash flows that are expected from it. Thus, if all wealth earned a 5 percent return, a 40 percent income tax would be arithmetically equivalent to a 2 percent wealth tax. Either would cost you $2 for each $100 of wealth.

5. The payroll tax applies to a legal definition of wages that does not, for example, include Bill Gates's stock appreciation. A further limitation to the measure of earnings that have been subject to payroll tax is that, until 1994, even the Medicare portion of the tax applied only up to an annual ceiling.

6. As Moon (1996, 164) notes, however, this might reduce "the crucial deterrent effect of cost sharing" on seniors' decisions to seek treatment, by causing the copayment to be collected some time after the healthcare service had been rendered.

7. Yet another possibility would be to means-test the Medicare eligibility age, requiring individuals with higher incomes to wait longer to enter the system. Such a rule would probably require significant advance notice, so that people planning to retire when they no longer needed the employer-provided health insurance would be able to plan. In addition, it would have to be structured carefully to minimize the resulting incentive to retire early so that one's income would be low enough to permit earlier eligibility.

8. If Medigap insurers nonetheless covered income-related deductibles, one might expect them to use information about enrollees' likely income (for example, prior years' tax returns) in setting their premiums. Otherwise, they would risk being subject to significant adverse selection.

9. On the possible advantages of "notches" in the tax system, see Blinder and Rosen 1985. For an example of an optimal income tax model in which marginal tax rates are lower for higher-income than for lower-income taxpayers, see Slemrod, Yitzhaki, Mayshar, and Lundholm 1994.

10. If an age-conditioned marginal tax rate increase seems unfair, consider that the generational redistribution it accomplishes is probably considerably less than that which resulted from initial enactment of Social Security and Medicare, to the benefit of contemporary seniors who never had to pay the taxes for these programs.

11. The fact that the income tax does not recognize unmarried, including same-sex, couples is a financial benefit for two-earner couples, who generally would pay higher taxes if forced to amalgamate their earnings on a joint return.

12. In illustration, consider the 1997 Senate Finance Committee plan, under which, for single enrollees, the Part B deductible would have increased from $100 to $540 when income reached $50,000, and then capped at $2,160 when income reached $100,000. Suppose that the plan had accomplished effective income-splitting by raising a married couple's combined deductible to $1,080 when the spouses' combined income reached $100,000, capped at $4,320 when their income reached $200,000. Spouses who earned $60,000 and $30,000 would avoid facing higher deductibles under the means test by reason of being married. By contrast, spouses who earned $150,000 and $50,000, respectively, would face a combined deductible of $4,320 in lieu of the $2,700 total that would have applied had they not been married.

Chapter Ten

1. The change in projected spending on Medicare and fighting terrorism might, however, affect one's views as to generational distribution. Suppose, for example, that the Medicare change implied a reduction in future enrollees' need for healthcare expenditure, while the antiterrorism change had to be borne over the next few years. The offsetting changes might suggest increasing current generations' resources at the expense of future generations.

2. Examples of consumption tax-style provisions in the current income tax are the exclusion of unrealized asset appreciation and the allowance of various exclusions and deductions for retirement saving.

3. To illustrate differences in transition incidence, suppose that my employment contract states that my annual salary under a multiyear contract is $100,000. For the duration of the contract, a 5 percent income tax increase would actually cost me $5,000 per year, whereas a 5 percent payroll tax increase, nominally split with my employer, would cost me only $2,500. This (reasonably) assumes, of course, that the contract does not explicitly address salary adjustments in the event of a tax law change.

4. See Shaviro 2001b, 61–62, for further discussion of the point that a consumption tax can be as progressive as an income tax so long as the rates are more graduated. Extra progressivity can also be changed on the transfer side of the fiscal system.

5. In practice, the retail sales taxes adopted by state and local governments in the United States generally to have more gaps in their application than, say, European VATs. They also apply at times to interbusiness transactions, leading to "cascading" tax liabilities unless the production process is vertically integrated (Gale 1998).

6. The cunning thing for Congress to do, if it had the political leeway, would be to specify the dedicated Part B financing as low initially and higher down the road. However, the initially dedicated percentage of income tax revenues would need to be set in such a way as to ensure that the Medicare Trust Fund would not officially run out before it increased.

REFERENCES

Aaron, Henry J. 1999. Medicare Choice: Good, Bad, or It All Depends. In *Medicare Reform: Issues and Answers,* edited by Andrew J. Rettenmaier and Thomas R. Saving. Chicago: University of Chicago Press.

———. 1991. *Serious and Unstable Condition: Financing America's Health Care.* Washington, D.C.: Brookings Institution Press.

———. 1966. The Social Insurance Paradox. *Canadian Journal of Economics and Political Science* 32:371–74.

Altonji, Joseph, Fumio Hayashi, and Laurence Kotlikoff. 1992. Is the Extended Family Altruistically Linked? Direct Tests Using Micro Data. *American Economic Review* 82:1177–98.

Antos, Joseph R. 1998. Preparing for the Retirement of the Baby Boomers. In *Medicare: Preparing for the Challenges of the 21st Century,* edited by Robert D. Reischauer, Stuart Butler, and Judith R. Lave. Washington, D.C.: National Academy of Social Insurance.

Antos, Joseph R., and Linda Billheimer. 1999. The Bumpy Road to Reform. In *Medicare in the Twenty-first Century: Seeking Fair and Efficient Reform,* edited by Robert B. Helms. Washington, D.C.: AEI Press.

Atkinson, Anthony B. 1995. *Incomes and the Welfare State.* Cambridge: Cambridge University Press.

———. 1987. Income Maintenance and Social Insurance. In *Handbook of Public Economics,* vol. 2, edited by Alan J. Auerbach and Martin Feldstein. Amsterdam: North-Holland.

Auerbach, Alan J. 1999. U.S. Fiscal Policy in a (Brief?) Era of Surpluses. Available at http://www.emlab.berkeley.edu/users/auerbach/.

Auerbach, Alan J., and Kevin Hassett. 2001. Uncertainty and the Long-Term Design of Fiscal Policy. In *Demographic Change and Fiscal Policy,* edited by Alan J. Auerbach and Ronald D. Lee. Cambridge: Cambridge University Press.

Auerbach, Alan J., and Laurence J. Kotlikoff. 1987. *Dynamic Fiscal Policy.* New York: Cambridge University Press.

Auerbach, Alan J., and William G. Gale. 2001. Tax Cuts and the Budget. Available at http://www.emlab.berkeley.edu/users/auerbach/ftp/auerbach-gale.pdf.

———. 2000. Perspectives on the Budget Surplus. *National Tax Journal* 53:459–72.

Auerbach, Alan J., William G. Gale, and Peter R. Orszag. 2002. The Budget Outlook and Options for Fiscal Policy. *Tax Notes* 95:1639–62.

Ball, Robert M. 1998. Reflections on How Medicare Came About. In *Medicare: Preparing for the Challenges of the 21st Century,* edited by Robert D. Reischauer, Stuart Butler, and Judith R. Lave. Washington, D.C.: National Academy of Social Insurance.

Barr, Nicholas. 1993. *The Economics of the Welfare State.* Stanford: Stanford University Press.

Bierce, Ambrose. 1993 ed. *The Devil's Dictionary.* New York: Dover Publications.

Bittker, Boris. 1975. Federal Income Taxation and the Family. *Stanford Law Review* 27:1389–63.

Blinder, Alan S., and Harvey S. Rosen. 1985. Notches. *American Economic Review* 75:736–47.

Boards of Trustees of the Federal Hospital Insurance and Federal Supplementary Medical Insurance Trust Funds. 2002. *Annual Report.* Washington, D.C.: Government Printing Office.

Board of Trustees of the Federal Hospital Insurance Trust Fund. 2001a. *Annual Report of the Federal Hospital Insurance Trust Fund.* Washington, D.C.: Government Printing Office.

Board of Trustees of the Federal Supplementary Medical Insurance Trust Fund. 2001b. *Annual Report of the Federal Supplementary Medical Insurance Trust Fund.* Washington, D.C.: Government Printing Office.

Bosworth, Barry P. 1996. Fund Accumulation: How Much? How Managed? In *Social Security: What Role for the Future?*, edited by Peter A. Diamond, David C. Lindeman, and Howard Young. Washington, D.C.: National Academy of Social Insurance.

Bradford, David F., and Daniel N. Shaviro. 2000. The Economics of Vouchers. In *Vouchers and the Provision of Public Services,* edited by C. Eugene Steuerle, Van Doorn Ooms, George Peterson, and Robert D. Reischauer. Washington, D.C.: Brookings Institution Press.

Brown, Randall S., Jeannette W. Bergeron, Dolores G. Clement, et al. 1993. *The Medicare Risk Program for HMOs — Final Summary Report on the Findings from the Evaluation.* Mathematica Policy Research, report to the Health Care Financing Administration.

Clymer, Adam. 1997. House Is Critical of Medicare Plan by Senate Panel. *New York Times,* June 20, A-1.

Coase, Ronald H. 1988. *The Firm, the Market, and the Law.* Chicago: University of Chicago Press.

Coate, Stephen. 1995. Altruism, the Samaritan's Dilemma, and Government Transfer Policy. *American Economic Review* 85:46–57.

Cohn, Jonathan. 2001. Second Opinion. *New Republic,* July 30.

Cutler, David M., and Louise Sheiner. 2000. Generational Aspects of Medicare. *American Economic Review* 90, no. 2:303–7.

Dowd, Bryan E., Roger Feldman, and Jon Christianson. 1996. *Competitive Pricing for Medicare.* Washington, D.C.: AEI Press.

Dranove, David. 2000. *The Economic Evolution of American Health Care: From Marcus Welby to Managed Care.* Princeton: Princeton University Press.

Engen, Eric M., and William G. Gale. 1997. The Effects of Social Security Reform on Private and National Saving. In *Social Security Reform: Links to Saving, Investment, and Growth,* edited by Steven A. Sass and Robert K. Triest. Boston: Federal Reserve Bank of Boston.

Epstein, Richard A. 1999. *Mortal Peril: Our Inalienable Right to Health Care?* Cambridge, Mass.: Perseus Press.

Feenberg, Daniel, and Jonathan Skinner. 2000. Federal Medicare Transfers across States: Winners and Losers. *National Tax Journal* 52:713–32.

Feingold, Eugene. 1966. *Medicare: Policy and Politics, A Case Study and Policy Analysis.* San Francisco: Chandler Publishing.

Feldstein, Martin. 1999. Prefunding Medicare. National Bureau of Economic Research Working Paper 6917.

———. 1987. Should Social Security Benefits Be Means-Tested? *Journal of Political Economy* 95:468–84.

Feldstein, Martin, and Andrew Samwick. 1997. The Economics of Prefunding Social Security and Medicare Benefits. National Bureau of Economic Research Working Paper 6055.

Feldstein, Martin, and Elena Ranguelova. 1998. Individual Risk and Intergenerational Risk Sharing in an Investment-Based Social Security Program. National Bureau of Economic Research Working Paper 6839.

Feldstein, Martin, and Jonathan Gruber. 1995. A Major Risk Approach to Health Insurance Reform. In *Tax Policy and the Economy 9*, edited by James M. Poterba. Cambridge: MIT Press.

Feldstein, Paul. 1998. *Health Care Economics*, 5th ed. Albany: Delmar Publishers.

Frech III, H. E. 1999. The Forgotten Opportunity of Reforming Fee-for-Service Medicare. In *Medicare in the Twenty-first Century: Seeking Fair and Efficient Reform*, edited by Robert B. Helms. Washington, D.C.: AEI Press.

Friedman, Milton. 1962. *Capitalism and Freedom*. Chicago: University of Chicago Press.

———. 1957. *A Theory of the Consumption Function*. Princeton: Princeton University Press.

Friedman, Thomas L. 1997. Oops! Wrong War. *New York Times,* April 7, A-15.

Fuchs, Victor R. 2000. Medicare Reform: The Larger Picture. National Bureau of Economic Research Working Paper 7504.

———. 1998a. Provide, Provide: The Economics of Aging. National Bureau of Economic Research Working Paper 6642.

———. 1998b. Health Care for the Elderly: How Much? Who Will Pay For It? National Bureau of Economic Research Working Paper 6755.

———. 1984. "Though Much is Taken"—Reflections on Aging, Health, and Medical Care. National Bureau of Economic Research Working Paper 1269.

———. 1978. The Supply of Surgeons and the Demand for Operations. *Journal of Human Resources* 13(supp.):35–56.

Gale, William G. 1998. Don't Buy the Sales Tax. Brookings Policy Brief No. 31. Available at http://www.brook.edu/dybdocroot/comm/policybriefs/pb031/pb31.htm.

Garber, Alan M., Thomas MaCurdy, and Mark McClellan. 1998. Diagnosis and Medicare Expenditures at the End of Life. In *Frontiers in the Economics of Aging*, edited by David A. Wise. Chicago: University of Chicago Press.

Geanakoplos, John, Olivia S. Mitchell, and Stephen P. Zeldes. 1998. Would a Privatized Social Security System Really Pay a Higher Rate of Return? National Bureau of Economic Research Working Paper 6713.

Glassman, James K., and Kevin Hassett. 1999. *Dow 36,000: The New Strategy for Profiting from the Coming Rise in the Stock Market.* New York: Times Books.

Glied, Sherry. 1997. *Chronic Condition: Why Health Reform Fails.* Cambridge: Harvard University Press.

Gokhale, Jagadeesh, and Laurence J. Kotlikoff. 1999. Medicare from the Perspective of Generational Accounting. In *Medicare Reform: Issues and Answers,* edited by Andrew J. Rettenmaier and Thomas R. Saving. Chicago: University of Chicago Press.

Gokhale, Jagadeesh, Benjamin R. Page, and John R. Sturrock. 1999. Generational Accounts for the U.S.: An Update. In *Generational Accounting around the World,* edited by Alan J. Auerbach, Laurence J. Kotlikoff, and Willi Liebfritz. Chicago: University of Chicago Press.

Graetz, Michael J., and Jerry L. Mashaw. 1999. *True Security: Rethinking American Social Insurance.* New Haven: Yale University Press.

Gruber, Jonathan. 1998. Comment. In *Inquiries in the Economics of Aging,* edited by David A. Wise. Chicago: University of Chicago Press.

Gruber, Jonathan, and Michael Lettau. 2000. How Elastic Is the Firm's Demand for Health Insurance? National Bureau of Economic Research Working Paper 8021.

Harsanyi, John C. 1953. Cardinal Utility in Welfare Economics and in the Theory of Risk-Taking. *Journal of Political Economy* 61:434–35.

Havighurst, Clark C. 1990. The Professional Paradigm of Medical Care: Obstacle to Decentralization. *Jurimetrics Journal* 30:415–30.

Himelfarb, Richard. 1995. *Catastrophic Politics: The Rise and Fall of the Medicare Catastrophic Coverage Act of 1988.* University Park: Pennsylvania State University Press.

Hoffman Jr., Earl Dirk, Barbara S. Klees, and Catherine A. Curtis. 2000. Brief Summaries of Medicare and Medicaid. Health Care Financing Administration, Department of Health and Human Services. Available at http://www.hcfa.gov/pubforms/actuary/ormedmed/.

Joint Committee on Taxation. 2002. *Estimates of Federal Tax Expenditures for Fiscal Years 2003–2007.* Washington, D.C.: Government Printing Office.

Jones, Stan. 1998. The Medicare Beneficiary as Consumer. In *Medicare: Preparing for the Challenges of the 21st Century,* edited by Robert D. Reischauer, Stuart Butler, and Judith R. Lave. Washington, D.C.: National Academy of Social Insurance.

Kahn III, Charles. 1998. Comment. In *Medicare: Preparing for the Challenges of the 21st Century,* edited by Robert D. Reischauer, Stuart Butler, and Judith R. Lave. Washington, D.C.: National Academy of Social Insurance.

Kaplow, Louis. 1998. A Note on the Optimal Supply of Public Goods and the Distortionary Cost of Taxation. *National Tax Journal* 51:117–25.

Kotlikoff, Laurence J. 2001. The Coming Generational Storm. Available at http://www.econ.bu.edu/kotlikoff.

———. 1995. *Generational Accounting: Knowing Who Pays, and When, for What We Spend.* New York: Free Press.

Kotlikoff, Laurence J., and Jeffrey Sachs. 1997. It's High Time to Privatize. *Brookings Review* 15:15–17.

Lee, Julie, Mark McClellan, and Jonathan Skinner. 1999. The Distributional Effects of Medicare. In *Tax Policy and the Economy 13,* edited by James M. Poterba. Cambridge: MIT Press.

Lee, Ronald, and Ryan Edwards. 2002. The Fiscal Effects of Population Aging in the US: Assessing the Uncertainties. In *Tax Policy and the Economy,* vol. 16, edited by James M. Poterba. Cambridge: MIT Press.

LeGrand, Julian. 1982. *The Strategy of Equality.* London: George Allen & Unwin.

Lichtenberg, Frank R. 2000. Sources of U.S. Longevity Increase, 1960–1997. CESifo Working Paper Series, No. 405.

Loomis, Burdett. 2000. The Politics of Vouchers. In *Vouchers and the Provision of Public Services,* edited by C. Eugene Steuerle, Van Doorn Ooms, George Peterson, and Robert D. Reischauer. Washington, D.C.: Brookings Institution Press.

Lubitz, James D., and Gerald F. Riley. 1993. Trends in Medicare Payments in the Last Years of Life. *New England Journal of Medicine* 328, no. 15:1092–96.

Luft, Harold, et al. 1990. Hospital Volume, Physician Volume, and Patient Outcomes: Assessing the Evidence. *New England Journal of Medicine* 298:1336–43.

Marmor, Theodore R. 2000. *The Politics of Medicare,* 2nd ed. New York: Aldine de Gruyter.

McCaffery, Edward J. 1997. *Taxing Women.* Chicago: University of Chicago Press.

McClellan, Mark. 2000a. Medicare and the Federal Budget: Past Experience, Current Policy, Future Prospects. Prepared for the NBER Conference on Tax Policy and the Economy, October 2000.

———. 2000b. Medicare Reform: Fundamental Problems, Incremental Steps. *Journal of Economic Perspectives* 14:21–44.

———. 1996. Medicare Reimbursement and Hospital Cost Growth. In *Advances in the Economics of Aging,* edited by David A. Wise. Chicago: University of Chicago Press.

McClellan, Mark, and Jonathan Skinner. 1997. The Incidence of Medicare. National Bureau of Economic Research Working Paper 6013.

Mirrlees, James. 1971. An Exploration in the Theory of Optimum Income Taxation. *Review of Economic Studies* 38:175–208.

Modigliani, Franco, and Richard Brumberg. 1954. Utility Analysis and the Consumption Function: An Interpretation of Cross-Section Data. In *Post Keynesian Economics,* edited by K. K. Kurihara. New Brunswick: Rutgers University Press.

Moon, Marilyn. 1996. *Medicare Now and in the Future,* 2nd ed. Washington, D.C.: Urban Institute Press.

Moon, Marilyn, ed. 2000. *Competition with Constraints: Challenges Facing Medicare Reform.* Washingon, D.C.: Urban Institute.

National Bipartisan Commission on the Future of Medicare. 1999. *Final Breaux–Thomas Medicare Reform Proposal.* Washington, D.C.: Government Printing Office.

Neufeldt, Victoria, and Andrew N. Sparks, eds. 1995. *Webster's New World Dictionary.* New York: Pocket Books.

Neumark, David, and Elizabeth Powers. 1999. Means Testing Social Security. In *Prospects for Social Security Reform,* edited by Olivia S. Mitchell, Robert J. Myers, and Howard Young. Philadelphia: University of Pennsylvania Press.

Newhouse, Joseph P. 2001. Commentary. In *Themes in the Economics of Aging,* edited by David A. Wise. Chicago: University of Chicago Press.

Newhouse, Joseph P., and the Insurance Experiment Group. 1993. *Free for All? Lessons from the RAND Health Insurance Experiment.* Cambridge: Harvard University Press.

Oberlander, Jonathan. 2003. *The Political Life of Medicare.* Chicago: University of Chicago Press.

Office of Management and Budget. 2002. *Budget of the United States Government, Fiscal Year 2003: Analytical Perspectives.* Washington, D.C.: Government Printing Office.

Patashnik, Eric. 2000. *Putting Trust in the U.S. Budget.* Cambridge: Cambridge University Press.

Patashnik, Eric, and Julian Zelizer. 2001. Paying for Medicare: Benefits, Budgets, and Wilbur Mills's Policy Legacy. *Journal of Health Politics, Policy, and Law* 26:7–36.

Pauly, Mark V. 1999a. *Health Benefits at Work: An Economic and Political Analysis of Employment-Based Health Insurance.* Ann Arbor: University of Michigan Press.

———. 1999b. Can Beneficiaries Save Medicare? In *Medicare in the Twenty-first Century: Seeking Fair and Efficient Reform,* edited by Robert B. Helms. Washington, D.C.: AEI Press.

———. 1999c. Should Medicare Be Less Generous to High-Income Beneficiaries? In *Medicare Reform: Issues and Answers,* edited by Andrew J. Rettenmaier and Thomas R. Saving. Chicago: University of Chicago Press.

Pear, Robert. 2001. Spending on Prescription Drugs Increases by Almost 19 Percent. *New York Times,* May 8, A-1.

Perry, Craig William, and Harvey S. Rosen. 2001. The Self-Employed Are Less Likely to Have Health Insurance Than Wage-Earners. So What? National Bureau of Economic Research Working Paper 8316.

Posner, Richard. A. 1995. *Aging and Old Age.* Chicago: University of Chicago Press.

Poterba, James M., and Lawrence H. Summers. 1986. Public Policy Implications of Declining Old-Age Mortality. In *Work, Health, and Income among the Elderly,* edited by Gary Burtless. Washington, D.C.: Brookings Institution Press.

Rauch, Jonathan. 1994. *Demosclerosis: The Silent Killer of American Government.* New York: Times Books.

Rawls, John. 1971. *A Theory of Justice.* Cambridge: Harvard University Press.

Reischauer, Robert D. 2000. Medicare Vouchers. In *Vouchers and the Provision of Public Services,* edited by C. Eugene Steuerle, Van Doorn Ooms, George Peterson, and Robert D. Reischauer. Washington, D.C.: Brookings Institution Press.

———. 1997. Midnight Follies. *Washington Post,* June 22, C-7.

Rettenmaier, Andrew J., and Thomas R. Saving. 2000. *The Economics of Medicare Reform.* Kalamazoo, Mich.: W. E. Upjohn Institute for Employment Research.

———. 1999a. Paying for Medicare in the Twenty-first Century. In *Medicare Reform: Issues and Answers,* edited by Andrew J. Rettenmaier and Thomas R. Saving. Chicago: University of Chicago Press.

———. 1999b. Saving Medicare. Dallas: National Center for Policy Analysis. Available at http://www.ncpa.org/studies/s222/s222b.html.

Riley, Gerald, Cynthia Tudor, Yen-Pin Chiang, and Melvin Ingber. 1996. Health Status of Medicare Enrollees in HMOs and Fee-for-Service in 1994. *Health Care Financing Review* 17:65–76.

Robinson, James C., and Patricia E. Powers. 1998. Restructuring Medicare: The Role of Public and Private Purchasing Alliances. In *Medicare: Preparing for the Challenges of the 21st Century,* edited by Robert D. Reischauer, Stuart Butler, and Judith R. Lave. Washington, D.C.: National Academy of Social Insurance.

Rosen, Harvey S. 1999. *Public Finance,* 5th ed. Boston: Irwin McGraw-Hill.

Samuelson, Paul A. 1958. An Exact Consumption-Loan Model of Interest with or without the Social Contrivance of Money. *Journal of Political Economy* 66:467–82.

Saving, Thomas R. 2002. Testimony before the House Budget Committee on Medicare and the Federal Budget (May 8). Available at http://www.house.gov/budget/hearings/saving02 .pdf.

Shaviro, Daniel N. 2002. Endowment and Inequality. In *Tax Justice Reconsidered: The Moral and Ethical Bases of Taxation,* edited by Joseph Thorndike and Dennis Ventry. Washington, D.C.: Urban Institute Press.

———. 2001a. Tax Simplification and the Alternative Minimum Tax. *Tax Notes* 91:1455–68.

———. 2001b. Some Observations concerning Multijurisdictional Tax Competition. In *Regulatory Competition and Economic Integration: Comparative Perspectives,* edited by Daniel C. Esty and Damien Geradin. Oxford: Oxford University Press.

———. 2000a. *Making Sense of Social Security Reform.* Chicago: University of Chicago Press.

———. 2000b. *When Rules Change: An Economic and Political Analysis of Transition Relief and Retroactivity.* Chicago: University of Chicago Press.

———. 1999. Effective Marginal Tax Rates on Low-Income Households. *Tax Notes* 84:1191–1201.

———. 1997. *Do Deficits Matter?* Chicago: University of Chicago Press.

Shiels, John, and Paul Hogan. 1999. Cost of Tax-Exempt Health Benefits in 1998. *Health Affairs* 18:176–81.

Shiller, Robert J. 2000. *Irrational Exuberance.* Princeton: Princeton University Press.

———. 1998. Social Security and Institutions for Intergenerational, Intragenerational, and International Risk Sharing. Prepared for the Carnegie-Rochester Public Policy Conference, April 24–25.

———. 1993. *Macro Markets: Creating Institutions for Managing Society's Largest Economic Risks.* New York: Oxford University Press.

Simons, Henry C. 1938. *Personal Income Taxation.* Chicago: University of Chicago Press.

Skinner, Jonathan, and Elliott Fisher. 1997. Regional Disparities in Medicare Expenditures: An Opportunity for Reform. *National Tax Journal* 50:413–25.

Skinner, Jonathan, Elliott S. Fisher, and John E. Weinberg. 2001. The Efficiency of Medicare. National Bureau of Economic Research Working Paper 8395.

Skocpol, Theda. 1998. Pundits, People, and Medicare Reform. In *Medicare: Preparing for the Challenges of the 21st Century,* edited by Robert D. Reischauer, Stuart Butler, and Judith R. Lave. Washington, D.C.: National Academy of Social Insurance.

Slemrod, Joel, and Jon Bakija. 1996. *Taxing Ourselves: A Citizen's Guide to the Great Debate over Tax Reform.* Cambridge: MIT Press.

Slemrod, Joel, Shlomo Yitzhaki, Joram Mayshar, and Michael Lundholm. 1994. The Optimal Two-Bracket Linear Income Tax. *Journal of Public Economics* 53:269–90.

Steuerle, C. Eugene, Edward M. Gramlich, Hugh Heclo, and Demetra Smith Nightingale. 1998. *The Government We Deserve: Responsive Democracy and Changing Expectations.* Washington, D.C.: Urban Institute Press.

Study Panel on Capitation and Choice. 1998. *Structuring Medicare Choices: Final Report of the Study Panel on Capitation and Choice.* Washington, D.C.: National Academy of Social Insurance.

Trivers, Robert. 1971. The Evolution of Reciprocal Altruism. *Quarterly Review of Biology* 46:35–56.

Tversky, Amos, and Daniel Kahneman. 1974. Judgment under Uncertainty: Heuristics and Biases. *Science* 185:1124.

Varian, Hal R. 1980. Redistributive Taxation as Social Insurance. *Journal of Public Economics* 14:49–68.

Vogel, Ronald J. 1999. *Medicare: Issues in Political Economy.* Ann Arbor: University of Michigan Press.

Weinstein, Neil. 1980. Unrealistic Optimism about Future Life Events. *Journal of Personality and Social Psychology* 38:806.

Weisbrod, Barton. 1991. The Health Care Quadrilemma: An Essay on Technological Change, Insurance, Quality of Care, and Cost Containment. *Journal of Economic Literature* 29:523–52.

INDEX